The Animal Within
The power of Maya Nahuales

ELISA FUSI

DEDICATION

Within your silence a whole universe commits to bring me home, in the splendour of blue ocean tide melting the depth of nocturnal notes. Sounds as gentle as caressing waves drip from the centre of your being. Sweetness speaks in a whirling pitch. Creeping pearls, vines of gems, shades of flames collapsing into cobalt whistles. Luminous flares everywhere.

Davide when you are close, a world of synesthesia explodes.

CONTENTS

Introduction   Pg 5

1   Animal Totem   Pg 6

2   Creation of Cosmo and Time   Pg 9

3   Myths, Legends and Gods   Pg 16

4   Maya Nahual   Pg 23

5   Understanding the Energy of the Day   Pg 61

6   Finding the Animal within   Pg 65

7   Animals in Dreams   Pg 69

Introduction

When contacting the wisdom of ancient Mayans one can be overwhelmed at the beginning by a sense of despair.

Plenty of information on symbolism and cosmology is available, but in order to enter the authentic Maya spirit, a great stretch of the mind is needed.

Mayans were truly connected to nature and the higher resonance of creation through rituals and ceremonies which, in current times, are poorly understood or completely misunderstood.

They were able to worship and honour animals and plants while at the same time brutally sacrifice human beings.

For them, time was neither linear nor aseptic and death was definitely a passage in time.

We know that most of those sacrifices were voluntarily performed during special occasions and many different techniques were used to reach ecstasy.

In Mayan medicine it is impossible to disconnect the world of spirit from the world of matter; it is therefore unconceivable to separate the dance of planets and stars from the ordinary life on earth. In fact, life on earth was not ordinary.

For this simple reason the symbolic language of poetry and dreams is used in the book to transfer to the reader their vision as it was in the purest form.

In order to start recognizing these patterns of wisdom, it is suggested to visualize concepts more than to analyse them with the rational mind.

The animal within is the primordial, archetypal sound of tribal drums that each one would easily hear immersed in the stunning silence of a forest or in dream realms.

Being faithful or not, the power of animals will follow us in this journey with a sense of renewal, foresight and endurance.

At our side and inside.

1 ANIMAL TOTEM

"Scientific thought and the miraculous unconscious are two waves in the same ocean."

Alejandro Jodorowsky

A fierce, elegant tiger, with her splendour and grace, is facing me in a room without walls. Her eyes are shining like a piece of charcoal, mirroring the vastness of the night. She appears in radiant flames and commands my attention.

"Do you come to devour me? Do you want to eat my flesh?" I should ask, but I don't. She's quiet and tremendously patient. She wants me to abandon any fear, any sense of imminent death. She wants me to communicate my state of being and then surrender. In dreams her and I speak and we are fellow companions. In dreams we melt and we tame the unconscious beast.

So how could I be scared? How could I feel my life is threatened?

Are you that luminescent wild thing flashing inside me?

We are the same aspect of a kaleidoscopic entity and you fight to emerge, gorgeous and proud. I swear.

Your breathe follows mine, we are matching the distant path that we embarked upon at the beginning of the ark collection. This collection full of colourful, blissful animals bridging my rebellious ocean, the tsunami of my unconscious mind, intensely crashing into the solid land of reality. Apparently solid, filled with bricks of memories and beliefs.

Reality cannot compete. The tiger moves forward with a soundless sound, she invites me into an invisible dance. Reality falls apart as I step onto the inexistence of the floor. Now I know there is nothing to dread. With the blink of an eye, we may growl together and walk along a road as sharp as a razor blade without being hurt when we accept each other in our hearts.

Beyond the substratum of collective consciousness, any animal in dreams can partially represent a pure conflict, a very personal limit or fear and it definitely represents an internal desire. The desire to be revealed, to be accepted or integrated in one's personality or simply a little reminder of an ancient fellowship. If we recognize a genuine universal meaning behind the animal totem, we also need to dismember it from the personal imagery. Indeed, they are interlaced but we cannot recall a symbol without all the outputs of our personal circumstances. A tiger could recall the sense of wilderness yet still transcend the pure act of love one moment after. To investigate dreams is to observe, after all. Observe the dream and the dreamer and actively question.

In such a dream, the dreamer can contact the ancient inner force of the tiger and proceed to the next level of comprehension. The animal provokes a reaction, feelings flow as a multitude of dimensions, inner dimensions that we can grasp one at a time.

The reality of spirit beings, totems and their assistance to those in the physical world has been a part of every major religion. The Greeks spoke to spirits and gods through oracles. Bushmen of Africa developed rituals and myths from the movements and activities of animals such as the eland and mantis. The Native Americans imitated animals in dance and rituals to establish links with the spirit realm. Belief in the spiritual realms of life and all of its varied manifestations is universal. The most common belief in many societies is that spiritual guides often use animals or animal imagery to communicate their purpose and roles to humans. In our modern, rational society there is a tendency to scoff at such possibilities. Spirit beings - whether in the form of saints, angels, ancestral contact, fairies and elves, demons, and animal totems - fill our ancient myths and scriptures. When beliefs are as universal as these, some attention should be given to them.

Some dreams are the result of a connection between our material selves and our spiritual Nahual or Maya guardian, and during these times, our personal Nahual may confer with other Nahuales, or with ancestors. The purpose of the investigation on Maya Nahuales is to help you strengthen your ties with the invisible world and eventually contact a deeper level of the Self through dreams and visions. As with any relationship, the better you know and understand your Nahual spirit, the more clearly you will be able to interpret what it is saying.

The Nahual is the link between a person and God (Ajaw). It is our spiritual companion or spiritual Self, created at the moment of conception, a companion that each person carries with them throughout their life. Establishing a closer relationship with this companion will allow you to hear them both more often and more clearly.

Each of the 20 Nahuales may relate to the dream of a person, in the same way that each day has meaning in the life of every human being. Some Nahuales may have more influence in our dreams than others. The Time Bearer (Cargador del Tiempo) of the present year will have influence, as will the Nahual of the current day. The four Bearers (Noj, Ix', Ee, Kej) fulfil an important role for the Maya, they are the Day lords who take responsibility for carrying the sun up from the underworld each morning, through the day and back into the underworld in the evening.

The change of the day is at midnight. If we dream a little before midnight, the dream is linked to that earlier day. When you record your dreams in your dream journal, remember to note the day and time the dream occurred.

In this sense, the dream can be viewed and interpreted as a conversation. Indeed, it is a conversation. You and your Nahual spirit are conversing. You bring your satisfactions and anxieties to the conversation with your Nahual, You unveil most of the subconscious facts. As with any conversation, those taking part bring not only their ideas but also their interests, their personalities, strengths and weaknesses, and unique ways of saying things. The better we know our conversation partners, the better we understand what they are trying to tell us.

Someone's unique way of conversing includes symbols and metaphors, the images we use to express complicated ideas and emotions. In dreams, our own subconscious mind might possess symbol images that our waking self finds confusing. Likewise, Nahuales may express themselves in symbolic ways. Many of these symbols, or dream elements, are somewhat universal and their meanings are shared between people.

2 CREATION OF COSMO AND TIME

"And while I stood there I saw more than I can tell, and
I understood more than I saw; for I was seeing in a sacred manner
the shapes of things in the spirit, and the shape of all shapes as they must live together
like one being."

Black Elk, Black Elk Speaks

Maya Cosmovision is a value system that interprets and connects the world, life, things and time. It envisions the origin of time and explains how to size Universe and Nature. The Cosmovision, through the Cholq'ij (Tzolk'in calendar) establishes the relationship between human beings and all the elements that surround him, with visible and invisible forces.

This way of explaining the world, life and things is defined as a cosmogonic interconnected and holistic vision. This vision is now an alternative to build a harmonious society with deep respect and human freedom. It is a philosophy of life that promotes the material well-being, but also the fullness of the spirit.

The Maya of Mesoamerica creation story is recounted in the sacred book, Popol Vuh.

The Popol Vuh, or Popol Wuj in the K'iche' language, is the story of creation of the Maya culture. Members of the royal K'iche' lineages that once ruled the highlands of Guatemala recorded the story in the 16th century to preserve it under the Spanish colonial rule.

The Popol Vuh, meaning "Book of the Community," narrates the Maya creation account, the tales of the Hero Twins, and the K'iche' genealogies and land rights.

In Maya mythology, Tepeu and Gucumatz (also known as Kukulkan, and as the Aztec's Quetzalcoatl) are referred to as the Creators, the Makers, and the Forefathers. They were two of the first beings to exist and were said to be as wise as sages.

Tepeu and Gucumatz held a conference and in order to preserve their legacy, they needed to create a race of beings able to worship them. Huracan, the god of storm, was the real creator while Tepeu and Gucumatz guided the process.

"In the beginning there were only sky and sea, personified as a trinity of gods called Heart-of-Sky. They decide that they want someone to praise them. They began by saying 'Earth', which appears from the sea. Earth was followed by mountains and trees, next the creatures of the forest were created; birds, deer, jaguars and snakes. They were told to multiply and scatter, and then to speak and pray. But the animals just squawked and howled. So Heart-of-Sky tried to make some more respectful creatures from mud. But the results were not desirable, and they allowed the new race to be washed away.

They called upon their grandparents, who suggested wood as an appropriate medium. But the wooden people were just mindless robots, so Heart-of Sky set about the destruction of this new race by means of a rain-storm. This caused the animals to turn against the wooden people; even their pots and querns rebelled, and crushed the peoples' faces. The wooden people escaped to the forests and were turned into monkeys. Heart-of-Sky then made another attempt at creating a suitably respectful race, and finally succeeded by fashioning humans out of maize-corn dough"

"Our Creation Story teaches us that the first Grandparents of our people were made from white and yellow corn. Maize is sacred to us because it connects us with our ancestors. It feeds our spirit as well as our bodies."

Juana Batz Puac, K'iche' Maya, Day Keeper

Another myth connects the creation with the god Huracan, who blew as a great wind over the primeval ocean, causing the earth to rise from the depths. Then Xpiacoc and Xmucane, "old man and old woman," performed magical rites that helped Huracan and other creator deities to form plants, animals, and eventually the human race.

"In the beginning was Silence.

From within Silence was born the Sound.

The Sound is the Son of Silence.

Within Silence was Sound."

(The 'Original Sound')

The first sound, the original vibration is symbolized in the Maya culture by the square within the circle.

It is the symbol of the Absolute Being, the Architect of the Universe, 'The Measure and the Movement'.

This event of the Birth of Time is also described, among others, by the Nada Brahma: Akasha is the ether or cosmic space where the original sound 'Om' was propagated. Also modern science, explaining the big bang theory recalls the event of creation as "the universe emerged from the 'void', at a single point called a singularity".

The first sound is represented by the square within the circle which defines the four directions needed to create a universe, a volume from the 'void'. This is the Mayan Cross, the Base of the Universe, the Compass.

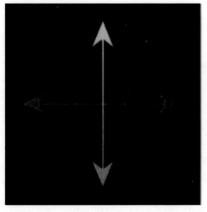

Mayan Cross and elements:

North-Air

South-Earth

West-Water

East-Fire

According to this vision all vibrations which constitute what we call 'universe': the planets, atoms, flowers, animals, humans, including the universe itself as a whole, are formed by this universal cell.

This is the harmony and movement of the four basic Elements.

The order of apparition of the Kin (Nahual sign), from 1 to 20, repeats the movement of the Mayan Cross; Fire, Air, Water and Earth which are connected with the Four Worlds.

"The First World was a world of solely the consciousness of the mineral Kingdom. It was a world directed by the guardians of the East, the red colour, and the Element of Fire. It was a silent gestation time. The Earth was mostly molten lava. Crystals were beginning to form in the Earth's crust. Nothing moved, since it was timeless and spaceless. There was only a recording of the blue print of life. Some of the crystals found today still maintain the encoding of this blueprint of life.

The Second World was the Kingdom of Plants and Minerals together. It was a world directed by the guardians of the North, the white colour, and the Element of Air. It was the wisdom of the blueprint put into action and the dimension of time. Algae began to grow and evolved into various plants. Time was born, and cycles of life and death began. You could feel life bursting forth and falling away. Some plants evolved from the minerals that had the blueprint of life encoded within them.

The Third World was the Kingdom of Animals, Plants and Minerals together. It was a world directed by the guardians of the West, the dark blue colour, and the Element of Water. Animals gained the ability to move about their environment, and dimension of space was born and linked with time within the blueprint. The world of the animals was instinctual. Animals knew how to thrive, but didn't know how to manipulate their environment. They lived with nature and in the present. All was acted upon instinctually based on the encoding in the blueprint. This world was the wisdom of the blueprint put into time and space with instinct. Some animals still carry the power of this blueprint.

The Fourth World is the world of Human Beings, Animals, Plants and

Minerals together. It is a world directed by the guardians of the South, the yellow colour, and the Element of Earth. This world was the wisdom of the blueprint put into time, space, instinct, but also consciousness. Animals evolved into Human Beings and began to gain the ability to change their environment. The Human Being could envision and plan for the future and learned to manipulate the blueprint. Humanity took its first steps in being consciousness beings with creative powers. They learned how to alter the blueprint. Humanity considered itself master of all worlds without respect for earlier worlds. Human beings have misused minerals, plants and animals. Also, guilt, fear, greed, lust, gluttony, laziness and hate were born: the seven deadly egos. The Fourth world is a world of creative force. Star seeding took place in this world to help to raise the consciousness of the human being. "

Beside this sophisticated concept there is another myth represented by the World Tree which separate the world in three layers: Heaven, the Middle World, and the Underworld.

Above: *Mesoamerican World Tree*

The roots of the tree are connected to the underworld, its trunk to the middle world, and its branches to the highest layer of the other world. The whole tree represents the Milky Way.

The Milky Way itself was celebrated by the Maya and they used to represent it by a tall and majestic flowering tree, the Ceiba also national tree of modern Guatemala.

The Milky Way was also called the Wakah Chan. Wak means "Six" or "Erect". Chan or K'an means "Four", "Serpent" or "Sky".

The Milky Way rose up from the horizon and climbed overhead into the North and the star clouds that form the Milky Way were seen as a place where all life began.

A major element of the World Tree includes the Kawak Monster, a giant head with a kin (symbol) in its forehead. This monster was also a mountain. A bowl on its head contains a flint blade representing sacrifice, and the Maya glyph that represents death.

On top of the World Tree we find a bird that has been called, the Principal Bird deity, or Itzam Ye. During the months of winter, when the so-called "Winter" Milky Way dominates the sky, it was called the "White Boned Serpent."

Another important symbol in Maya culture is the Hunab Kuthat is said to represent the Supreme God or the One Being, with 'Hunab' meaning 'one state of being' and 'Ku' meaning 'God.'

It encompasses all opposites in the universe and unites them as one: male and female, dark and light, yin and yang, conscious and unconscious, internal and external—the list goes on. Some believe that the Hunab Ku acts as a bridge to connect these opposites.

The Hunab Ku symbol is testament to the belief that it can unite opposite forces. It can be linked to the yin-yang symbol, with black spirals on one side, and white spirals on the other.

Above: *the Hunab Ku*

3 MYHTS, LEGENDS AND GODS

"They know all, what shall we do with them now? Let their sight reach only to that which is near; let them see only a little of the face of the earth! Are they not by nature simple creatures of our making? Must they also be gods?"

Popol Vuh

In Mayan mythology, the gods and heroes had many different names and appearances, stories occurred in varying forms, and scenes and figures changed and shifted with confusing rapidity. Beneath this seeming confusion, though, lay a sense that the universe was an orderly, structured place and that proper behaviour toward the gods played an important role in maintaining its harmony and balance.

The earliest known images of Mesoamerican gods were created by the Olmec civilization of Mexico. Emerging sometime after 1400 B.C., the Olmecs lived along the southern coast of the Gulf of Mexico for roughly a thousand years. They built pyramids that were sacred places where the human realm touched the realm of the gods. They also carved enormous stone heads as images of their leaders and created a long-distance trade network across Mesoamerica to obtain valued items such as jade.

The Olmec pantheon probably included deities of rain, corn, and fire, as well as a feathered serpent god. These figures reappeared in the myths of later Mesoamerican peoples. Olmec art included images of jaguars and of creatures that were part jaguar, part human. People of the region believed that magicians could turn themselves into jaguars.

The Zapotecs, Toltecs, and Aztecs were among the Mesoamericans who inherited and built upon Olmec traditions. So did the Maya, who were concentrated in the lowlands of Mexico's Yucatán Peninsula and in a highland region that extends from the present-day states of Tabasco and Chiapas into Guatemala. The Maya enjoyed their greatest wealth, power, and success from around A.D. 300 to 900. Historians call this their Classic period. During this time, the Mayas built vast stone cities and ceremonial centres such as Tikal and Palenque. After the Classic period, Toltecs from central Mexico arrived in the Yucatán and eventually merged with the Maya. Their influence shaped late Mayan civilization at Chichén Itzá and Mayapán.

MAYA GODS

AH PUCH

Ah Puch, often shown with decomposing flesh and a head like a skull, was the god of death and destruction. He brought disease, was associated with war, and ruled the lowest level of the Mayan underworld. The modern Maya call him Yum Cimil (Lord of Death).

He is also connected with the number ten and with the evil bird Muan, his messenger.

KINICH AHAU

The sun god was Kinich Ahau, sometimes said to be one aspect of Itzamná. He was often associated with jaguars.

Among other things, he is patron God of the number four. In this aspect he commands disease and has control over drought.

CHAC

The rain god, a major figure in all Mesoamerican mythologies, was called Chac by the Maya.

He was often portrayed as a fisherman or as a figure with the features of a fish or reptile. Like other Mayan deities, Chac could appear in four forms, each associated with a particular colour and compass direction.

IXCHEL

Ixchel, wife of the chief god Itzamná was goddess of fertility, pregnancy, and childbirth.

She invented weaving and is often connected with the rainbow. Although known as a moon goddess, she has earth aspects too and women still make pilgrimages to her shrines.

EK-CHUAH

Ek-chuah is the god of merchants and trades. He is known to be the patron of Cacao which was used as a currency.

He is usually depicted as a dark brown or black deity connected with wars.

ITZAMNÁ

The chief god of the Maya was Itzamná—ruler of the heaven, of day and night, and of the other deities. Itzamná was a culture hero, a figure credited with giving people basic tools of civilization, such as language and fire. Said to have been the first priest and the inventor of writing, Itzamná was also linked to healing.

KUKULCAN

Quetzalcoatl, the Feathered Serpent, called Kukulcan by the Maya, was also a figure of great importance throughout Mesoamerica. Among the Aztecs, whose beliefs are the best-documented in the historical sources, Quetzalcoatl was related to gods of the wind, of Venus, of the dawn, of merchants and of arts, crafts and knowledge. He was also the patron god of the Aztec priesthood, of learning and knowledge.

Cizin or Kisin (stinking one) is a minor god, related to death. He is linked in particular with earthquakes, which often strike Mesoamerica with devastating force. The ancient Maya depicted him as a dancing skeleton with dangling eyeballs. His opponent was the god of maize and vegetation, called Ah Mun and or Hun-Hunahpú, often shown with an ear of maize growing from his head.

Other important heroes and deities are reported in the Twin Hero Myth in which their twin heroes, Hunahpu and Xbalanque are depicted.

"Hunahpu (Blowgun Hunter-Solar) and Xbalanque (Hidden Sun-Lunar) were trying to make a garden but every time they cleared away the underbrush, the forest animals put it back again. Finally they caught a rat and held its tail over the fire, until it started explaining. The rat started talking. "Look, you are not cut out to be gardeners anyway. There's something you'd be better at. I'll tell you if you let me go."

The rat explained that their father and uncle had been great handball players and how they were cut out themselves to be great ballplayers. The rat said, "You just need the proper gear and I know where your father hid it before he was lost to the Underworld."

The boys got the gear and started playing, but were noisy about their playing so that the Lords of Death were affronted by their lack of humility. They sent messengers to summon the boys to a ballgame in the Underworld.

This was acceptable for the Twins who wanted to defeat the Lords of Death because they learned it was them who took their father. They allowed themselves to go through many challenging tests and ordeals so as to get to a place where they could finally kill the Lords of Death, the same ordeals their father experienced but had failed.

Near the end of their successful completion of the tests, Hunahpu made his first mistake. From his hiding place in the blowgun, he wanted to see if it was daylight, so he stuck his head out and a night- flying bat sliced it off.

The Lords of Death started the game using this brother's head for a ball. But his twin, Xbalanque, managed to fool the Lords and got his brother's head back and put it back onto him, and then replaced the head with a squash. The boys resumed the game and one, defeating the Lords of Death, and setting up the opportunity to destroy them.

The boys then sought their father, found him, but he was not up to the trip home. So they left him in the ball court, saying they would play ball regularly to pray for and honour all those who sought hope, knowing this would at last ease their father's heart forever. The boys, finished with their work, and no longer arrogant, accepted the light and shadow aspects of life and the complementary nature of their opposing personalities.

The Gods then intervened in not only helping them climb back to Earth's surface, but honoured them and gifted the world by making Xbalanque the Moon and Hunahpu the Sun. Then the pair departed Xibalba and climbed back up to the surface of the Earth. They did not stop there, however, and continued climbing straight on up into the sky. One became the Sun, the other became the Moon."

Above: *the Hero Twins*

They became the two complementary forces that must remain in balance for life to survive on Earth. They should remind us that every one of the millions of star molecules we are made of must be in balance with its complementary twin. This means we cannot over-identify with one force or the other because of ego fear or ego satisfaction or other needs of the ego. We must accept the dark and the light in ways that we know how to keep our solar and lunar aspects in harmony and not be split into one when we are better to be more with the other.

The origin of Sun and Moon is not always the outcome of a Marriage with the Earth. From Chiapas and the western Guatemalan Highlands comes the tale of Younger Brother and his jealous Elder Brethren: Youngest One becomes the Sun, his mother becomes the Moon, and the Elder Brethren are transformed into wild pigs and other forest animals. In a comparable way, the Elder Brethren of the Popol Vuh Twin myth are transformed into monkeys, with their younger brothers becoming Sun and Moon.

4 MAYA NAHUAL

"Weak or wicked, great or small, in men and in animal, resides the same omnipresent, omniscient soul. The difference is not in the soul, but in the manifestation."

Swami Vivekananda

In the Mesoamerican cosmology, the word "Nahual" means "moment of radiance." It refers to the essence or the spirit of a person, animal, or thing, living or dead. This spirit is believed to function as the protector of a person, animal, or plant. It is believed that human beings have an animal spirit counterpart, received at birth, which protects them as they walk through the path of life. The Nahual is thought to help individuals in reaching deep comprehension of their personal core and in keeping communication with all things, including the timing of dreams, the presence of certain animals, movements of air or planets, bird songs, and other sounds. For these reasons, the Mayan people maintain a great respect for nature.

Elders say that the Nahual can use its power for good or for evil, depending on its personality. No one can capture the Nahual; it escapes when it wants to and transforms into something else. During any rite of passage in life, one's Nahual will be present as a constant guidance.

We can see the Nahuales as interwoven energies; they are part of everything that exists and everything existing has its Nahual. Every single day has a different Nahual. Every rock, every mountain, every tree, every animal and every star has its own Nahual. The human being is not disconnected from this web. We are born ruled by a Nahual, and this Nahual also represents an animal, an altar, a flower, a tree or a mountain. This is the interconnection of the whole design, according to Maya Cosmovision. The Nahuales are part of us; they represent us and we represent them. The Nahual can represent a part of our body, an animal, a place, an idea or an event; the same Nahual can represent different things, but if we open our vision, we can see that this apparently opposite aspects are the same.

The Cholq'ij (also known as Tzolk'in) is compound by 20 energies, called Nahuales by the Great Grandfathers and Grandmothers, and each of them has 13 different frequencies. The combination of the 20 Nahuales and the 13 frequencies gives us 260 days, which relates to the human gestation and the number of different cell types that we have in our body. The numbers 13 and 20 are extremely important for Mayan spirituality, as they are the base of the Cholq'ij sacred calendar. This calendar of 260 days is the result of the combination of these sacred numbers.

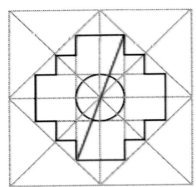

Left: *Inka cross, 13 squares and 20 corners*

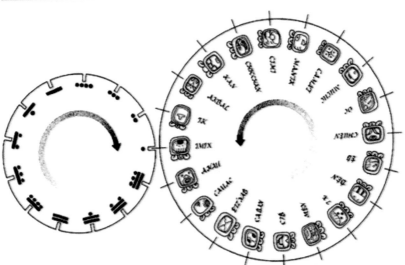

Above: *Maya Tzolk'in with 13 frequencies (ton) and 20 signs (kin)*

An old shaman (Ah-men) told me once that the Cholq'ij is the Human Calendar, representing the whole design of men. The human body has 13 articulations: neck, two shoulders, two elbows, two wrists, two hips, two knees and two ankles. It also has 20 fingers, magical tools given to us by our Creator, the great Ajaw (Ahau). The influence of this sacred frequency is not something that only the ancient Mayas were aware of. Other cultures in America share this same principle. The Tawa Chakana (the Inka Cross) contains in its shape the 13:20 frequency. It is important to remember that this symbol has influence over all South America.

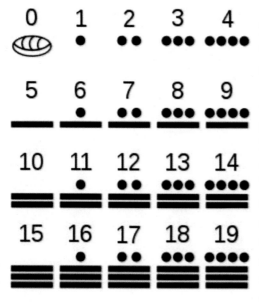

To better understand the Mayan calendar it is essential to explore the basic count and the underlying system.

Maya numerals were a vigesimal (base-twenty) numeral system used by the Pre-Columbian Maya civilization. The numerals are made up of three symbols; zero (shell shape), one (a dot) and five (a bar). For example, nineteen (19) is written as four dots in a horizontal row above three horizontal lines stacked upon each other.

The Haab' was the Maya solar calendar made up of eighteen months of twenty days each plus a period of five days ("nameless days") at the end of the year known as Wayeb'.(See Appendix II, page)

Each day in the Haab' calendar was identified by a day number in the month followed by the name of the month. Day numbers began with a glyph translated as the "seating of" a named month, which is usually regarded as day 0 of that month, although a minority treat it as day 20 of the month preceding the named month.

Neither the Tzolk'in nor the Haab' system numbered the years. The combination of a Tzolk'in date and a Haab' date was enough to identify a date to most people's satisfaction, as such a combination did not occur again for another 52 years, above general life expectancy.

Because the two calendars were based on 260 days and 365 days respectively, the whole cycle would repeat itself every 52 Haab' years exactly. This period was known as a Calendar Round. The end of the Calendar Round was a period of unrest and bad luck among the Maya, as they waited in expectation to see if the gods would grant them another cycle of 52 years.

The Mesoamerican Long Count calendar is a non-repeating almanac used by several Pre-Columbian Mesoamerican cultures, most notably the Maya. For this reason, it is sometimes known as the Maya Long Count calendar. Using a modified vigesimal tally, the Long Count calendar identifies a day by counting the number of days passed since a mythical creation date that corresponds to August 11, 3114 BCE in the Gregorian calendar.

Although the Maya and other Mesoamerican societies had the Haab', a solar year of 365 days, the Long Count is based upon a "mathematical year" of 360 k'in (days), called a tun, which means "stone" in Mayan. Twenty tuns (7,200 days) was a k'atun, which means "twenty stones." Twenty k'atuns (400 tuns or 144,000 days, or 394.3 solar years), constituted a b'ak'tun, meaning "a bundle of stones." Thirteen b'ak'tuns made up a Great Cycle, which adds up to 5,200 tuns and 260 k'atuns. All Long Count dates contain the following elements, written in this order: the b'ak'tun, the k'atun, the tun, the winal or 20-day period, and the k'in or day. A Mayan date such as 9.12.2.0.16 (July 5, 674 AD) means that 9 b'ak'tuns, 12 k'atuns, 2 tuns, 0 winals, and 16 k'ins have passed since the creation date.

The Long Count endowed the Maya with a sense of cosmic vision that made them unique. Though all Mesoamerican civilizations made use of the Sacred Calendar, only the Classic Period Maya practiced the Long Count.

Below: *The Long Count with glyphs*

K'IN 1 day						
WINAL 20 *k'in* 20 days						
TUN 18 *winal* 360 days						
K'ATUN 20 *tun* 7,200 days						
BAK'TUN 20 *k'atun* 144,000 days						
PIKTUN 20 *bak'tun* 2,880,000 days						
KALABTUN 20 *piktun* 57,600,000 days						
KINCHILTUN 20 *kalabtun* 1,152,000,000 days						

Whether or not they were the ones who invented it, they certainly adapted it as their own and made it one of the foundation stones of their culture. In a way, it is a measure of their unique mathematical and philosophical gifts.

Even if some modern Mayas look at their Nahual as a sort of horoscope sign, there is still a profound respect for the energy that a specific day is carrying.

Priests and shamans nowadays are using the count for observing special rituals of initiation, propitiation or wedding ceremonies. They recall the

Nahual and offer herbs, incenses or other symbolic meanings in order to be connected with the energy of the day.

THE TZOLK'IN

The body of the Tzolk'in calendar is the image of the Maya cross within it, the intention is expressing in 13 different tones, 13 Ton and its form is expressing in 20 different Nahuales, 20 Kin.

The different Kin and Ton combine with each other, creating the overall cycle of the Tzolk'in calendar composed of 260 beats: 13x20 = 260.

At each beat, a specific Ton and Kin mix together. They dance and court themselves and finally merge into a message.

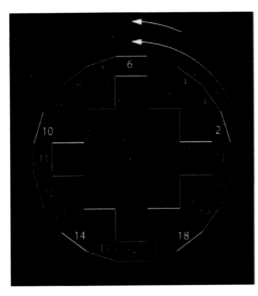

The order of apparition of the Kin, from 1 to 20, repeats the movement of the Mayan Cross; Fire, Air, Water and Earth.

The first expressing element is a Kin of Fire, symbol of birth and will. It appears, like the Sun, in the East.

The second element is a Kin of Air, symbol of the movement that creates the Spirit. It appears in the North.

The third element is a Kin of Water, symbol of the Inner World, Life and Emotions. It appears in the West.

The fourth element is a Kin of Earth, symbol of the Body and physical presence. It appears in the South. This cycle in 4 movements repeats 5 times in the same way allowing the manifestation of the 20 Kin of the calendar, 4x5 = 20.

Each Kin has its own name and glyph:

What we call 'Time' for Mayans is simply the child born at every moment from the romantic relationship between the universal masculine and feminine essences.

IMOX

Animal: Crocodile, Dolphin, Dragon, Fish
Force: The death initiation
Element: Fire
Colour: Red:
Direction: East
Body part: Blood
Opposite energies: Creation/Dissolution

Meaning: Primordial motivation, first thought, potentiality, latent energy, water. It is the root where everything comes from and where everything returns, creation out of nothing, motivation, activation of inner and occult power, change, eccentricity, sensibility, security, protection, spirituality, hypnotism, romanticism.
Insecurity, violence, dishonesty, egoism, exaggeration.
Energy that allows to create out of nothing.
Imox gives support, security and protection to new created elements such as life, idea, projects.

Ceremonial: Day to give, Day of therapists and healers.
The ceremonies which are carried out on this day aim to help persons charged or overwhelmed by negativity; as well they aim to reach healing people and thanking Mother Earth through offerings given to her.
It is an appropriate day to ask for rain; for the rivers to remain alive; for the wells and lagoons not to get dry. It is as well a perfect day to develop our internal powers.

Imox gives the spark of inspiration, it is connected to the primal creative forces, the zero as the fundamental latent energy that contains all possible realities. The idea seems to appear from nowhere, given by the motivation to create, the spirit of the heart, the divine communication.

The Imox is also the spirit of the rain. It favours the communication with the water animals, dolphins, whales.

The fixed farming calendar starts on a day Imox.

It is the symbol of the occult forces in the universe, manifested in madness and insanity. It is the day when the forces of Mother Nature became dangerous; at the same time, it is a day which settles the order as the balance in the mess and chaos. Imox is the name of all occult or secret things. It represents as well the left side, the left arm which mission is to help the right arm settle an efficient cooperation with the Heart of the Sky and the Heart of the Earth in the development and evolution of the world and humanity.

Imox represents the strength of our mind; it maintains the unity of all ideas. It is the original and telluric force, the melting pot of all where life appears. As well it is the perturbation of the human creations and actions, the confusion.

This sign offers an ability to treat mental disorders.

This day, we have to pay attention to set within ourselves a positive and centred balance.

IQ'

Force: Power of life, liberation
Animal: Hummingbird
Element: Air
Colour: White
Direction: North
Body part: Respiratory system
Opposite energies: Help/ destruction

Meaning: Wind, Breathe of Life, Blow.

Clarity, purity, move, change, inspiration, travel, liberty, spirit, harmony, purification, imagination, mathematical mind, caprice, communication, divination, signs.

Impulsivity, infidelity.

Iq carries new creations. It represents the movement of change, the dissemination of the seeds, the trust into creation. Iq gives the power to the life, it blows in new energy and blows out too heavy old thoughts, like the respiration of the body, the periodic tide of the sea.

Ceremonial: It is the day of the altars, of the air which is the sacred blow that gives us strength and fills us in with life. The ceremonies celebrated this day aim to thank the Sacred Mother Nature and the whole masterpiece of the Creator (Ajaw) for all that exists. During those ceremonies, it can be asked for the wind to take away with him all the sufferings, psychological traumas and illnesses.

As well, the day Iq' is appropriate for protection and for the growth of our spirit.

The air is the element which makes our body function; the element which gives us the motion.

Iq' is the spiritual and mystical breath; the vital principle. It is the essence of the existence of all living being.

The wind is the element which rules the ideas and the changes, it is the invisible space which exists between the material substances in our bodies; it is the window of the Mayan temples.

It is the destructive strengths of mankind and Mother Nature; it is imagination as well.

The wind is the inspiration and wisdom which comes from the highest source. Iq is the day of the Heart of the Earth which is the source of inspiration of the heart, and also the day of the Heart of the Sky which is the source of inspiration of the spirit, the cosmic vibration

Iq is a very powerful energy that can be either a smooth breeze of creation or a violent storm of destruction. It is also one of the bearers of time (cargadores del tiempo).

AQ'AB'AL

Animal: Guacamaya, Bat
Forces: the night, victory
Element: Water
Colour: Black or Blue
Direction: West
Body part: Stomach
Opposite energies: Light / Darkness

Meaning: Magic, vision, perspective, understanding, global view, divination, opportunity, luck, need of change, fun, laugh and joy, polarities, opposite forces and characters, resistance against negative power, trust, regeneration, juvenility.

Insecurity, fear, obscurity, duality, steal, irresponsibility

Aq'ab'al represents the night, the obscure, the unknown, the fears we have and the magic in the world.

It is the kingdom of darkness, the place where appear our deep fears. The real understanding of the world allows oneself to overcome his fears and bring the light of the truth.

Ceremonial: Aq'ab'al is a day of introspection. The ceremonies carried out on this day aim to thank for the radiant dawn and sunrise and for the crying, moaning, calumny and lie not to invade us. It is an appropriate day to ask for the dawn of peace and harmony for our peoples; as well to ask for the Light on the path and to ask for the occult things to be discovered. It is the day to ask for our sacred Fire not to get extinguished; also it is the day to ask for new opportunities of renewal of life, to put clarity on the mystery ; to ask for stability and a good work or business.

Aq'ab'al is the root of the world, it is the one which gives the opportunity to bounce from the bottom to the surface. It is the symbol of the dawn, sunrise; it is the sign that it is getting clearer, that the day is awakening and that the sunlight is ready for another day, a new era, a new lasting life which will take place on the blessed face of the Earth.

It is the symbol of the first rays of sun which come out, radiant on the horizon, keeping off and away the confusion, the ignorance; the gloom and darkness of the night. However, always there is a bit of light in the night and a bit of shade and darkness in the day; it is the duality of this sign.

Aq'ab'al means the most obscure of the night and the first ray of Light.

K'AT

Animal: Spider
Force: Attraction, Connection
Element: Earth
Colour: Yellow
Direction: South
Body part: Ribs
Opposite energies: Cooperation /
Oppression

Meaning: Connection, networking, communication, communion, gravity, memory, clarity, development, experience, abundance, offering, fecundity, emotion, spirit, sincerity, organization, order, intelligence.

Control, manipulation, egoism, trap, suffer.

Kat is the energy that brings things together. It can be seen as well as a prison, as a cohesion force that allows cooperation and brings the support for development.

Ceremonial: This day means the web, fecundity, tenderness, renewal, generic principle and wisdom. K'at is an appropriate day to solve a complicated matter and to celebrate a ceremony with a sacred fire. On the day K'at, it can be asked for the physical and mental development of children; also for the unity of the community, for the fecundity of women, for the withdrawal of the harming energies, for the undoing of the knots which attach us to vices, for solving emotional problems. It is also the day to pay to our ancestors.

K'at is the link which connects sacred places together. The shamanic network which links our world to upper and lower dimensions. It symbolizes the energy, the strength and the warmth in our hearts, from our first parents and this is what made their words transcend, their prayers and invocations for the world to be formed with beauty and harmony. As well it symbolizes the problems generated by ourselves or that our destiny puts on our way for our apprenticeship, growth and right evolution. It allows remembering, storing in our brain and mind, all that has been and is learnt. K'at is a very sacred and divine day.

KAN

Force: Intuition, Awakening
Animal: Serpent
Element: Fire
Colour: Red
Direction: East
Body part: Nervous system
Opposite energies: Peace / Anger

Meaning: Intuition, instinct, bright and fast, inner fire, move, change, action, connection between heart and spirit, spiritual development, knowledge, learning, teaching, justice, peace, influence, emotion, expression of the Self.

Egocentrism, manipulation, avarice.

Kan is the plumed snake, the one coming from the Earth with the ability to go into the Sky.

He is the messenger and link between the Earth and the Sky. It provides the missing element where it is needed. If the balance can restore a state of equilibrium, Kan is the energy which flows, it is the electric flow of the lightning. Capacity to change and to remember.

The snake symbolizes the connection with the intelligence of the Earth, the feminine part. The feathers symbolize the sky, the masculine part, the spirit. This energy gives solutions to problems trough intuition and instinct.

Ceremonial: It is the day of the truth. Kan is a good day to ask for good thoughts and good ideas. The ceremonies which are celebrated this day are to ask for justice, wisdom, strength, equality and for the balance in Mother Nature.
It is a good day to ask for the return of the beloved one, for the reconciliation, to ask for the couple.

Kan is the "Sovereign Plumed Serpent".The Quetzal Coatl, the Kukulkan, Tepeu, Quq Kumatz.
The ancestors used to say that we should observe how rivers run. The river journey evolves the same way as the snake.
The Snake is also in the air and forms great swirls; he is in the clouds when great showers get formed and there is the Hun Rakan or "Hurricane".
Kan can become very bad to the guilty, bringing illness, accident, hurricanes.
It symbolises the force of the universe, the warmth.
Kan is the movement, Creator of the universe, human evolution, spiritual development, justice, truth, intelligence and peace. Kan is the sign of wealth which multiplies the good things. It symbolizes agility too, wisdom of the elderly ones, integration, reunion. It represents sincerity, balance, power and authority.
It is a strong day. It is the energy of the fire which finds its root and base in the spine. It is the energy of the knowledge, the transmutation to wisdom, the strength and power of the snake, the sexual magic.

KAME

Animal: Owl
Force: Transformation
Element: Air
Colour: White
Direction: North
Body part: Physical death
Opposite energies: Rebirth /
Death

Meaning: Communication with ancestors, resistance against bad energies, movement and evolution of all that composes the universe.

Connection with other dimensions, spiritual power, law, life cycle, rebirth, trust, clarity, harmony, unexpected events, surprise, revelation, understanding, prudence, magnetism, charisma.

Death, anxiety, nightmare, aggressiveness, lie, fear.

Kame represents the cycles of reincarnations, the death and rebirth, the movement of evolution. The end of all things into death.

Ceremonial: It is the time of resynchronization, the total integration with the universal consciousness, the back to the roots, the rediscovering of the absolute reference. It is the day to remember ancestors.

It is the day to establish communication with the dead people and the live people.

It is the day of the reincarnation of the dead ones among the live ones. Our ancestors went for a rest; now, they are coming back to go on their mission on the Earth.

On a Kame day can be asked for knowledge, great wisdom from the ancestors. This day gives the understanding of what remains to be done and the energy to undertake it, he is the new try and the new opportunity.

Kame gives the opportunity for a new beginning based on a sudden understanding of things, like a vision or intuition. Kame, most important day among all the others, to pardon and ask for pardon for all the evil actions committed. The ceremonies celebrated on a day Kame are to ask for the rest of the dead people and to ask them for strength in order for them to be our spiritual guides and for them to accompany us during our journey of life on the face of the Earth, avoiding all danger, sickness and illness. It is an appropriate day to ask for strength and good memory for the success of our goals and projects. This day, the communication with superior beings is opened and the access to the dimensional doors is allowed.

Kame is the symbol of the final dissolution of all good and bad things, of death. It represents the beginning, the harmony, the vision, the smartness and intelligence. It develops the energy of the night to give light to another day.

Kame is the energy which advises us and protects us during all our existence through our ancestors. It forecasts the good and the evil. In the dimension of the dead people, there is no competition, no ambition, no sufferings and it is where we find the true peace and harmony.

Kame allows changes, replacing what is limiting, erasing the boundaries.

KEJ

Animal: Deer, Horse
Force: Protection, Support
Element: Water
Colour: Black or Blue
Direction: West
Body part: Hands
Opposite energies: Creation /
Destruction

Meaning: The Base of the Universe. Stability, resistance, connection with nature and outer world, physic-mental-emotion-spirit balance, responsibility, protection of nature, romanticism, speech, message, advice.
Shyness, hard character, culpability, pride.

Kej is the energy of realization. The physical process which creates new element in the nature.

It is the time to accomplish what is needed for subsistence.

Kej connects the four cardinal directions into potentialities like the four fingers with the thumb.

Kej is the connection between the physical and mental world, he is the four pillars of the universe, the four legs of the deer and horse. He is the transformer of the physical world from mental vision.

Kej is the guardian of the nature and living entities. Sacrificed elements have to be respected and thanked to balance the Universe.

Ceremonial: it is the day of physical action. Kej is an appropriate day to carry out ceremonies of initiation to become Ajq'ij (spiritual guide).

The ceremonies which are celebrated are to ask for strength, to ask for gestation, healing and protection of people.

Wajxaqib' Kej (8 Kej), is the day of the commemoration of the dead people; it is the day to thank our ancestors for all that we have inherited from them, for the possessions and especially for our spirituality. It is as well the day of commemoration of the ceremonies which have been carried out from the beginning of the world by our first ancestors, since nowadays. Kej also symbolizes the resistance, the physical power and the road of life. It is the time to prove power, courage and resistance. It is one of the four bearers of time.

It symbolizes the day of the human being as main authority and guide of the village and community. It means the strength and the power which bears the destiny of humanity. It represents the four supports, the four pillars and the four cardinal points which were created from the beginning to carry with strength and energy.

It refers to the 4 strengths of Mother Nature; the elements which nourish life : the Sun, the Earth, the Air, the Water ; the 4 Balams.

It is the sign in charge of the woods, forests and of Mother Nature; of the balance between human beings and Mother Earth; it is solidity and stability. It is all kinds of beings of four legs.

It is the service with humility, the vision of what is coming; it is a highly positive sign.

Q'ANIL

Animal: Rabbit
Force: Regeneration,
Fecundation
Element: Earth
Colour: Yellow
Direction: South
Body part: Ovary, Spermatozoid
Opposite Energies:
Generosity/Egoism

Meaning: The Regeneration of the Earth. Love, Seed, abundance, message, wish, harmony, intuition, responsibility, travel, spiritual power, community work, fertility, restart, life cycle, change and evolution, inner tranquillity and security, understanding.

Pride, superiority, egoism, discordance.

Q'anil is the guardian of the seeds, associated with Venus, the big star, symbol of love and fecundation, the abundance of life.

Q'anil expresses the human realization, it helps the Warrior in his travel to self-realization, to accomplish his destiny. He is associated with the cycle of life, death and rebirth. It brings the inner power to express the personality and potentialities.

Ceremonial: Q'anil is the time of harvest and celebration of the crops. There is a close connection with the kin Kej, the sow and the harvest. The ceremonies which are celebrated on the day Q'anil are carried out to thank all that Mother Nature brings to us: plants, life, rain, our food. It is an appropriate day to thank for the sowings and the harvests; to ask for children, animals to evolve in harmony; also, it is a good day to overcome the difficulties that poverty causes. It is as well an appropriate day to reconquer or take back something that is believed lost, it is a day of understanding. It is the day of good beginning.

On the day Wajxaqib' Q'anil (8 Q'anil), day of the blessing, we can ask for good sowing, good harvest, as well for animals not to harm or damage our crops. It is an appropriate day to ask for our shyness to get away; it is the day of the pregnant woman; the day to ask for the renewal, rebirth of sterile lands.

The day Kab'lajuj Q'anil (12 Q'anil) is a good day to offer and ask from all our heart to the Creator for the well-being in life.

Q'anil is the day associated with plants and all the live beings which have seeds. It is the divine semen, the cosmic seed planted on this planet.
It symbolizes the four colours of the corn (yellow, red, black and white).
It is the fertility of human beings, plants and animals.

TOJ

Animal: Puma
Force: Sharing, Offering
Element: Fire
Colour: Red
Direction: East
Body part: Ear and hearing
Opposite energies: Balance /
Correction

Meaning: Paying, the Universal law of Cause and Effect. Balance, take and give back, transparency, unity, liberation, community service, peace, connection with the Earth and the Cosmos, communication, movement, magnetism, energy, fertility, emotion.

Impulsiveness, worries, culpability, possessiveness.
Toj is the offering time in order to balance the universe. What has been taken has to be replaced or given back.

Ceremonial: The day of the offering. Toj is a day to thank and ask, for the well application of justice; to protect the life of persons easily subject to accidental deaths. This day, one can make an offer for the prevention of illnesses, difficulties and for the liberation from any negative energy. One can ask to pay for past lives and for no obstacle to be put on the way.
One can thank for everything that was given. The life, the food, the air, the water, fire and earth. Music and chants can be paid as an offering.
Toj protects and supports the creatures that can remember and feed their gods and symbolizes the sacrifice, the transparency in the world.

It is a warm sign and as well magnetic and sensitive. It is the day of payment to the Creation, to Mother Earth, to the Universe and to all the elements.
Toj means as well Tojil, when the Balams gave their offerings tothe rising Sun, to thank the new dawn, the new beginning; it is the sacred ceremonial fire.

T'Z'I

Animal: Dog
Force: Orientation
Element: Air
Colour: White
Direction: North
Body part: Instinctive brain functions
Opposite energies: Purity / Impurity

Meaning: Orientation, justice, fidelity, order, help and advice, light on truth, authority, concentration, strategy, attention, instinct, positivism, prosperity, material and spiritual life.

Manipulation, individualism, infidelity.

Tz'i' symbolizes the spiritual law and the authority.

Tz'i' shows the right action to do, the correct behaviour, how to act in life.

Ceremonial: The ceremonies which are carried out on a day Tz'i' are for the negative forces not to triumph, and for the authority to get mysticism, vision and understanding for a good application of the justice; to beg for pardon for the unnecessary thoughts; for the wrong use of the resources coming from Mother Nature. Tz'i' is a day to ask for solutions to legal problems and also for being in spiritual and material balance.

Kablajuj Tz'i' (12 Tz'i'), day of the midwife.

Tz'i' is the law, the authority, the justice, the faithfulness and the order. It is the interpretation of the known and unknown.

These authorities are the first parents (ancestors) who gave us those laws, based on the harmony of Mother Nature. They find their energy in natural places like the altars or pyramids.

With transparency and value of the word, Tz'i' is the perfect companion, the one who can be trusted, the one who helps.

B'ATZ'

Animal: Monkey
Force: Creativity
Element: Water
Colour: Black or Blue
Direction: West
Body part: Veins, Arteries
Opposite energies: Trust / Doubt

Meaning: The Master of the Arts. Creativity, imagination, spiritual connection, vision, future, evolution, infinite time, unity, community service, resolution of problems, arts, motion, humanity, life, sensibility, emotion, superstition, luck.
Pride, arrogance, insecurity, unexpected actions or events.
Bat'z' is link of time from the past to the future, it is the beginning of the story that will end in Tz'i'. Symbol of continuity of the past.

Ceremonial: Good day to ask for all humanity; to ask for crops, sowings; beginning of a project. Day to carry out any kind of activity with success: good day for the union of a man and a woman in a marriage. Day of offering, strength of the weavers. The origin of the World. In the requests of this day, we ask for a good life for all the creatures we all are, on the face of the Earth.

Wajxaqib' B'atz' (8 B'atz): date of revelation and formation of the human being. Iit is the new year of the Mayan Calendar.

Bat'z' could be a sign of inspiration but needs to acknowledge his opposite principle and overcome it. As Tzi'kin, the eagle, Bat'z' is living on top of trees and therefore can get the gift of spiritual vision. This detachment from earthly life gives the ability to create all kind of arts.

Bat'z' is the lucky day. The luck given to the beginner to motivate him to continue along his path. The boost that creates the path of destiny.

Bat'z' is the laugh that gives relative importance to the events that occur.

It symbolises the oldest brother. In the Mayan Mythology, the first divine twins were Jun B'atz' and Jun Chowen, older brothers of Jun Ajpu and Ixbalamke, who were defeated because of their selfishness and pride.

B'atz' is the time, the time in motion and evolution, the infinite time, the spirituality, the creator of life and wisdom. It is the beginning of intelligence and the evolution and human life.

It is the thread of time. The thread of destiny. In this thread are written all the events occurred all through the 5200 years of the Long Count. B'atz' as well is the thread or umbilical cord, the one which links us to the belly of our mother when we are being born. B'atz' as well is the thread with which our clothes are weaved, the beautiful "huipiles" which are the clothing of identification of the Mayans, and which bear a lot of their history.

That day B'atz' was established in order for the destiny of each one of us to be fulfilled. The one born on this day, has as his vocation to become an Ajq'ij, or spiritual guide. He will be a good spiritual guide, a messenger; he will lead a long life. The gifts which he possesses, that the Ajaw has manifested to him in his life, will be all the material that he possesses in order to heal at a material level and at a spiritual level.

EE

Animal: Lynx
Force: Wisdom, Guidance
Element: Earth
Colour: Yellow
Direction: South
Body part: Feet, Teeth
Opposite energies: Road /
Obstacle

Meaning: Sacred path, experience, road, travel, ancient knowledge, destiny, energy of action, free will, realization, power, seeking of originality and novelty, conciliation.

Distortion of reality, envy, manipulation, lie, infidelity, jealousy.

Ee symbolizes the road, the destiny, the ladder, the steps of consciousness.

Ee is the free will of humankind to start the quest of self-realization. Human has received the gift of free will to have the choice and power over his own destiny.

Ceremonial: This is the day of Destiny. This day, requests for good food, for protection of the sowings, for physical and mental wellbeing are made. Ee is the strength, the potential and the energy for the beginning of a labour, a trip, a journey. It is the Day of the fire in the shelter, of the plants, of the stars, of the sky. It is the Day of the personality and the material goods. It is the guide and protector of the traders.

It is the sacred path, the White Path.

Wajxaqib' Ee (8 Ee): day of memorial of life and fortune of each person.

Ee is the feeling of the Liberty of life, the feeling you have when you have reached the top of the mountain and you enjoy the view around you. This is the feeling of knowing that everything is possible, with no limit, the absence of fear and attachment.

The Ee guides us on the right way in order to accomplish our mission, the one for which we were born, such as being a good teacher, a good leader. The one born this day has the vocation of Ajq'ij (spiritual guide), someone who helps and guides with good examples in the material, as well as in the spiritual.

This day shows you, compels you to be polite with the people who surround you and with people in general. You have to love and know how to respect the elderly people, the teachers and the authority.

Ee will protect and clear the road of life, gives opportunities and luck during the travel. Ee constitutes one of the four Bearers of the Time because of its close relationship with nature.

AJ

Animal: Armadillo
Force: Multiplication
Element: Fire
Colour: Red
Direction: East
Body part: Spine
Opposite energies: Development /
Introversion

Meaning: Sky Walker, Cane. Multiplication of all things, life, spiritual development and consciousness. Abundance, love, multiplication, development, connection with trees and earth, power, harmony, unity, Inner fire, community, integrity, honesty, purity, morality, sacred words, the origin, simplicity, justice, emotions, authority, perfection, social projection. Instability, sadness, anger, introversion, obsession, indifference and pride.

Aj is the energy of multiplication.

The ability of everything to grow and replicate itself to create the diversity of life. An ocean of forms, shapes, colours that compose nature. The experience of life throughout infinite manners and characters.

Ceremonial: Aj is the Day of protection; it is a day to help the twins and to ask for the survival and life of Humanity.

Wajxaqib' Aj (8 Aj): day of celebration of ceremonies to ask for the protection of the new born babies and of the adults. Aj is the protector of the childhood in particular. It is the day of renewal, purification, rebirth, steadiness; it represents the origin, the profession or work, the constant blossoming of the existence and its development for the reaching of the bliss of life.

Aj is the Rod or sacred wrapper, the stick of power. In the Mayan language, it is called the A'j Chamiy'll.

The A'j chamiy'll is the great grand-father. From his lips flow words of encouragement and consolation, poetical words harvested in the fields; it is as if he would cut a flower from the field and plant it in his garden; the flowers being the metaphor of human beings.

It symbolizes all that is related to the shelter and the family. It is a symbol for the sowing of the cane which Jun Ajpu and Ixb'alankej made in the courtyard of the house of the grand-mother Ixmukane. It symbolizes the victory of life upon death. Aj symbolizes the victory upon all kinds of evilness, and it is as well a symbol for resurrection.

The name of Aj was given to this day as a symbol for the necessity of the first grand-parents for food, it is the day when the sacred corn and the animals were domesticated.

It represents the spine, the internal fire which moves and activates the secret powers. It is the spine and the link between the Earth and the Sky. It is the return to the shelter as the place of origin. It personifies integrity, honesty and rightness.

It represents the cane plantation, the seven virtues (fire, water, air, land, heart of the Sky, heart of the Earth and the centre) of the divine power, the clairvoyance, the telepathy, the corporal language and signs, the unexpected dreams.

Aj is an explorer, a researcher, trying all possibilities, all directions.

As universe is a living entity with an own personality, Aj is the expansion and development principle.

I'X

Animal: Jaguar
Force: Magic
Element: Air
Colour: White
Direction: North
Body part: Muscles
Opposite energies: Occultism / Materialism

Meaning: Woman, Magician. Occultism, mysticism, unknown, magic, feminine energy, connection with nature and spirits, shamanism, spiritual wealth and material poverty, inner experience and feeling, discovering of new abilities, sensibility, bravery, courage, resistance.

Mood, pride, egocentrism, envy and ambition.

I'x symbolizes the Heart of the Earth, the unconsciousness and the matter as one.

The unconsciousness is the fertile ground that allows spirit to grow, as the Earth for the plant.

I'x is the invisible, the mystery the unknown. It gives the power of creation of life out of nothing. Ix is the jaguar, the feminine principle that creates fertility for human, animals and plants.

Ceremonial: The ceremonies carried out on this day are to ask for pardon and forgiveness for the exploitation done to Mother Earth and its nature. It is a day to ask for protection against any kind of negative energy. It is an appropriate and favourable day to thank the work of women. It is a special day to ask for the good life of wild and domesticated animals. It is the appropriate day to ask for good crop and wisdom. It represents the Mayan Altar, all sacred places; it is the day of the mountains, summits and plains.

Wajxaqib' I'x (8 I'x) is the day to thank, the way our first grand-parents did it from the beginning of the world; it is the day to thank for our shelter, for the Earth that has been acquired, by heritage or by purchase.

6 I'x is the day of the Earth, the place where a being is born, where a being lives and where the family lives.

Ix is the Nahual of the shamans, the ones who travel through different levels of consciousness, and know the Primal Language, the universal communication tool that allow to speak with animals, plants, mountains.

It is the symbol of the creative forces of the universe, of the memorial of the World. It is the day when the Waters got separated from the mountains, from the plains and from the places occupied by human beings and all the animals of the Earth.

It is the day of the Higher Magic: this energy develops the superior Powers, intermediary between the visible and the invisible.

I'x symbolizes our mother, our woman, the mother of our children.

TZ'IKIN

Animal: Eagle, Birds
Force: Divination, Vision
Element: Water
Colour: Black or Blue
Direction: West
Body part: Eyes, Vision
Opposite energies: Luck / Misery

Meaning: Vision, dreams, liberty, global consciousness, divination, intuition, mysticism, independence, luck, magnetism, understanding, idealism, authority, arts, imagination, joy, eccentricity, communication. Intuition, visions and revelations in dreams.

Anger, lack of memory, irresponsibility, envy, exaggeration and egoism.

Tzi'kin symbolizes the ability to see beyond the decor.

It gives the detachment and altitude to see the surroundings with perspective. The vision comes from the Heart of the Sky, it is the comprehension, the light on the road, the idea.

Ceremonial: It is the perfect day for love and to ask for individual and communitarian abundance. Celebrations and offerings which are carried out and given on a day Tz'ikin aim to improve the wealth, to ask for simplicity and gentleness. As well, it is a perfect day to ask for common projects, for the protection in businesses, for the couple, the friendships and to move away the birds prejudicial to the sowings, especially to the Corn.

Tzi' kin shows the direction to go to, he is the divination, the reading of the future as a logical development of the story based on the present and past. It symbolizes the day when the birds showed the place where the Sacred Corn would be found. It is the representation of all that exists in the space.

It is the day dedicated to the Heart of the Sky, Heart of the Earth; it symbolizes the good fortune, luck and material stability; as well the consciousness and individual intelligence.

It is the intermediary between the Divine and the human being. The vision brought by Tz'ikin is wide; it is the panoramic and sure vision of the eagle. It is the guardian Bird of all the lands of the Maya area.

AJMAQ

Animal: Bee, Insects
Force: Intelligence
Element: Earth
Colour: Yellow
Direction: South
Body part: Aura
Opposite energies: Morality / Cheat

Meaning: Warrior. Heart of the Earth, wisdom, trust, connection with ancient knowledge, spirituality, philosophy, important message, intelligence, forgiveness, introspection, reflection, sagacity, feeling of infinite inner world.

Indiscipline, lie, jealousy, irresponsibility, infidelity, hard character

Ajmaq symbolizes the connections from and to the brain. It is the spirit, the communion with the other Nahuales, the moral force, the ability to acknowledge its own mistakes, the wisdom, the pure spirit of the warrior.

Ceremonial: On this day, we ask for the peaceful rest of the passed away and their role of intermediaries for the offenses and sins committed, not to happen again.

Ajmaq is the most appropriate day to forgive and be forgiven. It is the day to cure all types of illnesses; it is the day when the family problems can be solved; a day to ask for material and spiritual strength. As well, Ajmaq is the day of Harmony with Mother Earth. It is the symbolic day of the moral strengths. In the classic Mayan World, Ajmaq was the day when people asked for forgiveness to Mother Earth for all the mistreatments and abuses generated on her by people.

On the Jun Ajmaq (1 Ajmaq), ceremonies are carried out to thank for the sons and daughters; ask for their health and long life.

Ajamq is the messenger of the sacred past, the memory of the Earth, it represents the wisdom of stones and old trees.

It is the lessons of the ancestors, the remembering of past lives.

NOJ

Animal: Coyote
Force: Cosmovision
Element: Fire
Colour: Red
Direction: East
Body part: Brain
Opposite energies: Communion / Individualism

Meaning: Synchronicity, movement, intuition, connection with the All, selflessness, intelligence, adaptation, integration, perceptions, balance, clarity, wisdom, communication, loss of knowledge for the discovery of talent.

Individualism, inflexibility, vanity.

Noj is the intelligence, the ability to integrate its environment, the heart and energy of the thinking and knowledge.

It is the manner to perceive the universe, to synchronize with it.

Ceremonial: The energy of the No'j influences overwhelmingly the spirit and the mind of its bearers. In order to well orientate and positively develop this gift, it is advised to consult the Wise Persons. The No'j is the perfect day to ask for clarity, clairvoyance in order to transform the knowledge and the experiences into wisdom.

The ceremonies which are celebrated on that day are to request for good knowledge, good thoughts, good behaviour, and good memory; also the energy of the No'j is excellent to unify ideas; to unify intentions, to guide society on the good ways and to ask for what we need in life.

N'oj is idea and wisdom, name of our thoughts, form or set mode of behaviour. It symbolizes the ambivalent moral strengths in the human mind. It is the energy which rules the mind, the knowledge, the good memory. It is synonym of creativity and good talent. It is the day of decisions taking and of advice.

It is the connection of the spiritual Cosmic Mind with the human being mind. The ancestors used to meet up in council under the protection of the sign No'j in order to transform the knowledge and the experiences into wisdom and to actualize, adapt the receiving through and in the sciences.

The nobility is the major virtue brought by the energy of the No'j, in particular patience, prudence, cautiousness and love from higher dimensions.

Noj will advise in how to manage a new project, it will give the movement, the behaviour, the talent to realize it. No'j is one of the four Bearers of the Year.

TIJAX

Animal: Owl, Toucan, Swordfish
Force: Healing, Light
Element: Air
Colour: White
Direction: North
Body part: Teeth, Tongue Opposite
Elements: Inner World/ Outer
World

Meaning: The Fractal Vision, Loss of Ego. Selflessness, transparency, integrity, harmony, spiritual liberation, connection with stones and crystals, control, navigation, justice, bravery, intuition, talent, lightness, collaboration, compassion.

Egocentrism, sadness, danger, insecurity, possessiveness, jealousy.
Tijax is the obsidian knife, the principle of sacrifice.
Tijax is the mirror, the reflection from outside to inside and inside to outside. The understanding and realization of the fractal character of the world.
Tijax is the feeling of transparency, the integration of the whole, the dissolution of the ego into realization, understanding.

Ceremonial: Tijax is a day of purification and balance of our actions. It is a day to ask for good health, to cut with the enemies and maintain them away; it is an excellent day to ask for intelligence and memory.
The ceremonies celebrated this day have the goal of protecting from evil and accidents; keeping them away and preventing them. It is a day to cure physical and mental illnesses; as well it is a day to protect domestic animals

from illnesses. The spiritual guides born a day Tijax are the ones in charge of offering the Toj (the present to the Ajaw on the Mayans Altars).

Tijax is the obsidian stone, also called flint. It is the material that our ancestors used in order to carry out invisible operations.

This day orders us, guides us and forbids us. It is the Nahual of the healers, doctors. It is the sigh of the strong, brave and courageous persons; of the persons who collaborate, who are friendly and loving. It reflects flexibility in space and time.

It is the cutting, the separation, the knife, the healing and harmonising in the four bodies. The Tijax brings the power of cutting, solving, bringing to light all the mysteries. As well, this sign opens a road to other dimensions and realities.

KAWOQ

Animal: Turtle
Force: Strength
Element: Water
Colour: Black or Blue
Direction: West
Body part: Heart
Opposite energies: Justice / Dispute

Meaning: Community, family, feminine energy, fertility, valour, nobility, imagination, divination, guidance, dream, abundance, security, justice, collaboration, authority.

Intractability, clumsiness, culpability.

Kawoq is the energy of change, the Nahual of the storms, the disputes, the discharge of unbalanced situations.

Kawoq is related to Kan, it is intuitive, violent. It is the time after which the peace returns, it is perceived as a bad day but in fact it is not. As the water of the river is going from up to down, Kawoq just restores the tensed element into harmony, it brings everything back together.

Kawoq gives the energy to change things, it is the detonator, the last drop that makes the glass overflow.

Ceremonial: Kawoq is a special day in which the Ajq'ij (spiritual guide) carry out ceremonies of offering in order to ask for the sun to illuminate and warm up, for the well-being of the people, for the health of the ill persons, for the end of the conflicts and problems, and for the courage of the wand of authority to triumph. Also, this day, one can ask for wisdom in the use of medicinal plants and favourable weather for the growing and crops.

It is the day of the mediators, defenders, judges. It is the day of the value of the pole of authority; day of the woman who warms up the heart of the shelter with her maternal love. It is the energy which brings the rains in order to obtain good harvests. Kawoq is synonym of fecundity, versatility, music, painting and imagination.

It is the day of the energy of nature and of the elements.

It means the strength of the union, the expansive consciousness, the growing, the fertility and the children.

AJPU

Animal: Human
Force: Understanding
Element: Earth
Colour: Yellow
Direction: South
Body part: Chest Opposite
Energies: Everything/Emptiness

Meaning: The Sun, The Victory. Universal understanding, full realization, security, spiritual Warrior, Human being, power of life, fertility, infinity, knowledge, wisdom, integration of the world, friendship, guidance, wish, message, origin.

Egocentrism, individualism, doubt, anger, irresponsibility.

Ajpu is the time of the victory, the time before the new birth, the completion of the cycle.

Ajpu symbolizes the Mayan zero which is in the same time the All and the Nothing. It is pure potential, opportunities to realize. It is the seed and the Wish of Life.

Ceremonial: It is the day to ask for wisdom in order to understand the knowledge of the elders, more experienced and wiser people than us. It is the day to receive divine and natural messages, to ask for the maternal milk, to ask for the healing of illnesses; to ask for helping children improve their oral communication ability and as well to ask for strength for the weak ones.

The ceremonies carried out on a day Ajpu have to be as strong as the Sun in order for the illnesses, the calumnies to be pushed away. It is the day which gives strength, courage and energy to overcome the obstacles.

It is a very powerful day that brings the liberation, the solution to the problem and gives the strength of the Warrior.

Ajpu also symbolizes the infinite power, the universal understanding, the immortality, the integration of the World. It is the fusion of love and spirit, the male and female principles, the full integration.

It represents the musicians, artists, observers, communicators and writers.

It is the triumph upon the negative energies, the spiritual warrior. The twins Jun Ajpu and Ixbalamke defeat all the challenges and obstacles in Xibalba, the underworld; they die and resurrect; allegory of the spiritual awakening.

This sign bears material and spiritual certainty; it is the transformation and mutation; the one who carries out miracles. It is the intervention of the ancestors responding to the requests asked for during a ceremony. It is the physical strength; the strength to go on living after death.

5 UNDERSTANDING THE ENRGY OF THE DAY

In order to complete the exploration of the Tzolk'in it is essential to know the meaning and use of the Galactic Ton. The 13 Ton represent the masculine expression and the intention of the day, its motivation, and energy. The 13 numbers follow each other in the movement of a wave are represented in a pyramid shape; ascendant numbers from 1 to 6 connect to growth, ton 7 is the plateau or balance, descendant numbers from 8 to 13 connect to transformation.

The 13 numbers alternate following the numerical order (1 to 13).

Each time we are back to number 1, a new trecena then starts and always on a different glyph.

As it is the case for a wave, at the beginning the energy is weak (ton 1), almost undetectable, it becomes more powerful afterwards. The wave amplifies, raises, attaining its utmost strength (ton 7), then it starts to decrease in power until it reaches ton 13.

As a wave finishes, another one starts and rises, carrying another energy. The odd numbers are defined day, light, action and evolution energies and the even numbers are defined night, dark, restful and resistance energies.

The following paragraph gives, in synthesis, the ton with the conveyed energies, meaning and application.

TON 1

UNITY. Day of action. Definition of the new objective, choice of the intention. Also called the magnetic tone of purpose, it represents the attunement to the wave's goal to attract the energies necessary for its realization. The first day is the overall theme of the wave. It allows union with the source and magnetizes energies that push and guide us through the 13 days of the wave.

TON 2

DUALITY. Reaction. Balance between Intention and reality, revelation of problems, conflicts. Also called the lunar tone of challenge, it stands for sharp turns, duality and difficulty.

TON 3

ACTION. Creativity, quest of the harmonic between intention and its opposite. Also called the electric tone of service, it represents focus, flow and movement toward a solution to the challenge. This energy speeds up, operates and teaches to use the qualities of inspiration within us for ourselves and society.

TON 4

STABILITY. Setting the limits, formation of the body. It represents seeding possible solutions to the challenge by their exact definition. Teaches how to plant forms of accomplishment in reality and thus progress toward the solution to the challenge. Also called the independent tone of the form.

TON 5

EMPOWERMENT: Organization, support, detachment. It gives perspective. Also called the will power, it symbolises the heart centre.
It allows to gather and focus our energy and consequently to glow and radiate light in all directions.

TON 6

FLOW. Transformation, movement, integration of the intention in the real context. It is the rhythmic tone of balance and represents a balance with nature and the universe and a flow in space and time.

TON 7

REFLECTION. It is the balance at full growth. Connection with the physical path, vision of the whole, divination. The resonant tone of the attunement, it signifies the peak of the wave's intent and a direct contact with the source.

At the height of the wave, we refine our intention and channel it to production.

TON 8

HARMONY. Synchronization, Justice. Called galactic tone of integrity, it symbolizes harmony between the words, thoughts and actions – between deeds and the high reality, reinforcing loyalty to ourselves.

It teaches how to build the quality of integrity that is embodied in all of us, thereby increasing the harmony in our lives and in our world.

It allows merging with subtle vibrations and in creating a harmonious reality.

TON 9

PERSEVERANCE. Right action, new birth. Also called solar tone of intention, it represents the turning point of the wave and leads to a focused intent that moves, drives and fill our creation.

It allows the completion of the personal process and the completion of major energy cycles.

TON 10

MANIFESTATION. Also called planetary tone of manifestation, it signifies fulfilment and change of awareness following the recognition of the wave's completion of the process.

This is a day of gift, which teaches the perfection that exists in creation just as it is.

TON 11

RESOLUTION. Rationalization, simplification. The tone reflects the release and symbolises the renunciation of the old, breaking of patterns and releasing of beliefs that are no longer relevant to our lives.

TON 12

COMPREHENSION. Stability, understanding. This is the tone of cooperation and represents the solution to the challenge, the consolidation of poles rate and the learning of the wave's main lesson.

It teaches how to cooperate in meetings and in creation with the understanding that the whole is greater than the sum of its parts.

TON 13

ASCENSION. Openness to new consciousness, emergence of new opportunities. Also called cosmic tone of presence, it symbolizes the ability to be present at any moment and to resonate beyond the physical reality.

It unifies all the ends of the wave and leads to a universal change, to rest and to tune towards the new wave.

The table below is a summary of the 13 ton.

Tone			Mayan Name	Action	Power	Essence
1	•	Magnetic	Hun	Attracts	Unify	Purpose
2	••	Lunar	Ca	Stabilizes	Polarize	Challenge
3	•••	Electric	Ox	Bonds	Activate	Service
4	••••	Self-Existing	Can	Measures	Define	Form
5	—	Overtone	Ho	Commands	Empower	Radiance
6	•̄	Rhythmic	Uac	Equalizes	Organize	Equality
7	••̄	Resonant	Uc	Inspires	Channel	Attunement
8	•••̄	Galactic	Vaxac	Models	Harmonize	Integrity
9	••••̄	Solar	Bolon	Realizes	Pulse	Intention
10	═	Planetary	Lahun	Produces	Perfect	Manifestation
11	•̿	Spectral	Hun Lahun	Releases	Dissolve	Liberation
12	••̿	Crystal	Ca Lahun	Universalizes	Dedicate	Cooperation
13	•••̿	Cosmic	Ox Lahun	Transcends	Endure	Presence

6 FINDING THE ANIMAL WITHIN

When calculating our Nahual we need an almanac reporting Gregorian dates translated into the Tzolk'in calendar. If we don't have one there are simple and accessible calculators available online. After a person's main day sign has been determined, a simple calculation is used to find the other four Nahuales in the five-sign chart, called the Tree of Life or Mayan Cross.

Before proceeding to the next step, it is convenient to learn how to draw our Mayan cross. The Cross indicates the energies that govern the conception and destiny, and the left and right sides of the person. The Maya Cross represents the 4 corners of the universe, the four cardinal points.

In the Mayan cross there are four addictional rulers, which define: the conception, destiny, action and feelings.

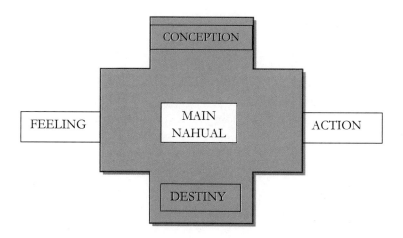

The conception represents the energy at the moment of your creation and deals with the essence of the individual, the core. It points the natural forces which shaped the inner Self.

The destiny is considered the unfolding of your path and the guardian in charge for the change, the transformation and the resolution.

Most Ah'men image the left side of the cross to be the emotional drive, the fuel and the way the world is perceived. It represents the feminine side.

The action ruler is the one guiding you to the fulfillment of your main nahual, a sort of tool for comprehension and subsequent removal of obstacles and fears. For some Mayans it represents manifestation and matter.

Therefore, one should always remember that the cross is connected with the four directions and the elements.

For a better comprehension of the cross, it is necessary to write in order the glyphs as they appear in the calendar, then write down the ton of your nahual and add the number in series.

In the table, the main nahual is 10 Ee. From this basic data one can obtain the rest of the rulers and also the trecena ruler, which is the first nahual (with the ton 1) starting the wave, in this case 1 Aq'ab'al.

To know the conception nahual one should count up to 9 from the main nahual (including this in the count) backward.

The conception nahual of the example is 2 Kat.

To know the destiny, one needs to count from the main nahual (icluding this in the count) afterward.

The destiny nahual results to be 5 Ajpu.

For the left side of the cross, one should count up to 7 afterward from the main nahual and obtaining the ruler of feelings which is 3 Tijax.

By counting up to 7 backward, the action ruler is found and in the example is 4 Kame.

Now the cross can be drawn as follows:

Nahual: 10 Ee

Conception: 2 Kat

Destiny: 5 Ajpu

Action Nahual: 4 Kame

Feelings Nahual: 3 Tijax

Some elders report 4 more Nahuales (constellations or corners) to add to the cross. They can be considered as multiple guardians during one's life, but are not included in the book since they are not common.

IMOX	12	
IQ'	13	
AQ'AB'AL	1	
KAT'	2	- 9 CONCEPTION
KAN	3	
KAME	4	- 7 ACTION
KEJ	5	
Q'ANIL	6	
TOJ	7	
TZ'I'	8	
B'ATZ'	9	
EE	10	MAIN NAHUAL
AJ	11	
I'X	12	
TZ'IKIN	13	
AJMAQ	1	
NOJ	2	
TIJAX	3	+ 7 FEELINGS
KAWOQ	4	
AJPU	5	+9 DESTINY

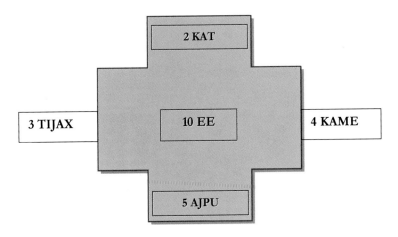

Above: *the complete Mayan Cross*

7 ANIMALS IN DREAMS

"Dreams are today's answers to tomorrow's questions."

Edgar Cayce

Likewise in the past, in contemporary Maya religion, dreams are considered sacred. They are seen as a powerful portal, a meaningful gateway to establish a connection with Ajaw (the highest Maya divinity) and also with the ancestors.

In order to guide the individual, dreamsmay reveal the unfolding path by shifting shapes and playing with concepts, carrying an unconventional message at that time when your soul can leave the physical body and travel far away.

By focusing on curative,guiding and sacred qualities, the interpretation of a dream can virtually embrace any ancient and recent form of Shamanism including the vast Mayan phylosophy. In fact, dream interpretation is a surviving art that although has evolved through psychology, is still alive in the world today.In Contemporary Maya spirituality, sleeping and dreaming are more than justthat ordinary, nightly ruitine that everyone takes part in. Dreams are not just randomthoughts that your brain chemistry moves on the surface while your body rests. Dreams indeed connect you with your profound, hidden Self.

"It is in dreams where you hear the voice of Ajaw and your ancestors, who guide you,warn you of danger, teach you and look out for your health and well being. Dreams tell you your destiny, your nawal, your calling.", elders say.

Dreams are real.

Ancient concepts of the alter-ego and the spiritof the individual that is active when dreaming, is seen in ancient Mayan art, referencedin Ancient Mayan Glyphs, and played a major role in the history of the ancient Mayans.

Michael D. Coe and Mark Van Stone explain the ancient term of the "Way", anindividuals´ co-essence, which usually took the form of a mixture ofmultiple animals. This concept of the Way existed mainly for theelite in the ancient Mayan civilization. Coe further explains that the word way also translates to "sleep" in some Mayanlanguages, and thus continues that "it is possible that such mystic contacts were made indreams," especially considering that some glyphs indicate "certain Classic buildings as"sleeping places," where maya kings may have sought out these spirits" (Coe, 2005). These sleeping places, called "Wayi or Waybil", were either the place where one went to sleepto connect with the Way, or a place where the Way lived. Also for the Yucatec people the Way (or Vaai) word means literally "enchanted transfiguration", mostly a transformation into an animal, while the Lacandon people of Mexico use the word "Way-al" for metamorphosis.

Modern Maya shamans sometimes use the word Way to refer to the journey of the vital force (Ch'ulel) out of the body during the dreaming state. Especially in the lowlands of Guatemala and in Alta Verpaz, shamans recognize the power of the Camuhuil, a small anthropomorphic stone images, which are frequently either kept on their domestic altars or in sacred bundles as intermediary in dreams. They serve as helpers in curing rituals or in transmitting knowledge through visions.

Likewise Mayans, traditional peoples of all Latin America believe that no important event ever occurs in a person's life unless it has first been dreamed.

According to Michael Harner in his "A core Shamanic Theory of Dreams", in Shamanism a special attention is paid to the 'Big Dream', considered as a great manifestation of the guardian spirit and appearing in form of a vision, an overwhelming waking dream or a recurrent sleeping dream. In both cases the dreamer encounters a materialization of a mindful message along with information that can be precious for the community and for the individual.

It is through dreams as well that the innate shamanic power was revealed in the majority of Native Americans' tribes. The animal guardian is said to appear during the initiatory dream and to transfer teachings on healing, hunting and other powerful instructions.

In parallel, the visionary states of the shaman provide information and integration processes that link our ancient animal brains into cosncious awareness. This is an integration of dream processes and their synthetic visual representations into consciousness through rituals. Dreams occurring within a ritualistic environment reflect the ability of altered state of consciousness in producing brain integration at many levels, as we see in the patterns of synchronized and coherent theta-wave discharges.

Animal totems or guardians commonly help the shamans in clarifying a doubt, in recognizing a latent need or desire and they may transfer specific powers to the dreamer. These metaphorical connections are still alive in our times and can be interpreted even without a guide. In the core shamanism it is fundamental for the dreamer to work with the inner voice and comprehend, deeply comprehend the language of dreams in a exclusive way. There is no one except the dreamer able to quest, investigate and intimately relate to the source of visions.

Even if universal interpretations are available for each Nahual or Animal Totem, one should always wonder what is the feeling provoked, which kind of bond merges and what the animal personally represents.

Common sense and a poetic mind will rapidly guide the dreamer to link a personal perspective to the general meaning and find the unique answer.

However, it can be helpful to understand the deeper, archetypal significance of the animals in your dreams as the genre of different species tend to carry within them certain attributes that all humans recognize. For instance, if Western people are asked what words or feelings spring to mind when they think of a dog they will often use words like pet, man's best friend, loyal and faithful. For sure, Maya will find other concepts culturally associated with this animal, like alertness and justice.

In the same way, an eagle will be universally associated with powerful sight and elegance, and a jaguar associated with agility and strenght. When involving animals it is important to ascertain whether your dream animal recalls a past experience or if it is there as an archetypal motif. It may actually be there for both reasons.

Though, it is advisable to first explore your own personal associations to the dream animal before investigating its mythical and archetypal qualities.

In the following paragraph some of the most common animal totems are reported along with shamanic view, Mayan interpretation and mythical or archetypal meaning.

HAWK (Eagle, Falcon)

The messenger of the spirit world
Power of focus, to see, clear vision
Strong connection with spirit, increased
spiritual awareness

"Great Sky Hunter,
teach me patience as you drift on thermals high above.
Teach me timing, as you dive with folded wings.
Teach me accuracy, as you strike with talons spread.
Lend me your vision, that I might find my prey at great distance.
Lend me your speed to capture that which I most desire.
Lend me your grace, that I might dance with each moment in life's headlong flight.
Let us soar and spin and plummet as one in the sky of existence. "
Falcon Prayer

In numerous traditions, the hawk has a strong relationship with the world of the gods. Some of this symbolism has persisted in modern mythology and beliefs. In Ancient Egypt, the belief was that a hawk-headed spirit called "Ba" would fly off a mummy to come back among the living as a hawk or swallow. The hawk symbolized a part of the soul that would be freed up after death and come back to the world of the living in the shape of a bird. It was also the animal of choice for the god Horus, god of the sky, who was represented with a hieroglyph depicting a falcon or hawk.

The popular belief in more modern times that birds like hawks or owls are announcer of death may be rooted in this myth. For the Greeks, the hawk and the eagle were associated with the god Jupiter, king of the gods. The bird is strongly connected with the realm of the gods.The hawk belong to the realm of bird medicine. It carries the symbolism that comes with the ability to fly and reach the skies.can soar high and reach the heavens effortlessly. The hawk is also a bird of prey. When you have the hawk as a spirit animal, you may have a natural inclination to receive visions, either in dreams or awake. Your extra sensory abilities and intuition are supported by the power of this animal.

The hawk totem is strongly connected to the spiritual realms. When it shows up in your life, you may be called to pay attention and experience rapid spiritual development.Having this animal as a spirit guide emphasizes your ability to lead and influence others.

Hawks symbolize the power of observation. This spirit animal's guidance may also indicate that you have the opportunity to study a situation before taking action. Observe the situation and then act when the time is right.

This totem could reinforce the ability to rely on intuition and spiritual guidance.

Maya Nahual: Tz'ikin

Tz'ikin is the intermediary between the sky and the earth, between god and man/woman.It signifies the guardian bird for all the land in the Maya area. In dreams it gives precognition and revelation.

HUMMINGBIRD

Lightness of being, enjoyment of life
Independence
Swiftness, ability to respond quickly
Resiliency, being able to travel great distances tirelessly

"Hope" is the thing with feathers -That perches in the soul -
And sings the tune without the words -
And never stops - at all —
And sweetest - in the Gale - is heard -And sore must be the storm -
That could abash the little BirdThat kept so many warm -
I've heard it in the chillest land -And on the strangest Sea -
Yet - never - in Extremity,
It asked a crumb - of me."
Emily Dickinson

Hummingbirds are found only in the Western hemisphere, so they are absent from the traditional fairy tales, legends, and myths of European and African people. There is, however, a rich supply of stories about these tiny birds in Native American mythology.

A Mayan legend says the hummingbird is actually the sun in disguise, and he is trying to court a beautiful woman, who is the moon.

Another Mayan legend says the first two hummingbirds were created from the small feather scraps left over from the construction of other birds. The god who made the hummers was so pleased he had an elaborate wedding ceremony for them. First butterflies marked out a room, then flower petals fell on the ground to make a carpet; spiders spun webs to make a bridal pathway, then the sun sent down rays which caused the tiny groom to glow with dazzling reds and greens. The wedding guests noticed that whenever he turned away from the sun, he became drab again like the original gray feathers from which he was made.

A third Mayan legend speaks of a hummingbird piercing the the tongue of ancient kings. When the blood was poured on sacred scrolls and burned, divine ancestors appeared in the smoke.

A Native American legend tells of a primordial time when people lived in an underground world of darkness. They send a hummingbird up to look for light. High above them the little bird found a twisted path to the sunlit upper world where people now live. In a Cherokee story, a medicine man turned himself into a hummingbird to retrieve lost tobacco plants.

Hopi and Zuni legends tell of hummingbirds intervening on behalf of humans, convincing the gods to bring rain. Because of this, people from these tribes often paint hummingbirds on water jars. The Hopi kachina for Hummingbird depicts him with green moccasins and a green mask. He has a water body, and he is yellow on top of the head.

The Pueblo Indians have hummingbird dances and use hummingbird feathers in rituals to bring rain. Pueblo shamans use hummingbirds as couriers to send gifts to the Great Mother who lives beneath the earth.

The hummingbird is one of the most fascinating birds because of its ability to move its body swiftly, change direction quickly and smoothly, seemingly gliding from one place to another. The hummingbird is known for burning a lot of energy quickly to keep flying and therefore needs to find sources of food constantly. By affinity with this power animal, you can be encouraged to use or develop a similar skill. The call of the hummingbird totem will guide you to open up to love and lightness in your emotional life.

Maya Nahual: Iq'

In dreams can represent a sudden change and the call for sweet sensuality.

DRAGONFLY (BUTTERFLY)

> Renewal and transformation
> Adaptability
> Realm of emotions
> Connection with nature's spirits
> Fairies and entities
> The psyche

"May the wings of the butterfly kiss the sun

and find your shoulder to light on,

to bring you luck, happiness and riches

today, tomorrow and beyond."

Old Irish Blessing

To the Japanese, the dragonfly symbolizes summer and autumn and is admired and respected all over, so much so that the Samurai use it as a symbol of power, agility and best of all, victory.

In China, people associate the dragonfly with prosperity, harmony and as a good luck charm.

Amongst Native Americans, it is a sign of happiness, speed and purity, because the dragonfly eats from the wind itself.

In European folklore, calling the dragonfly the witches' animal and that Satan sent it on earth to cause chaos and confusion, to calling it, Ear Cutter, Devil's Needle, and worst of all Horse Stinger. The name Horse Stinger comes from the misinformed observation that horses that were kicking and stamping around usually had a few dragonflies hovering around them.

In Sweden, folklore suggests that we dragonflies come around to check for bad souls, to weigh souls to be more 'accurate', believed to sneak up to children who tell lies and also adults who curse and scold, to stitch up their eyes, mouth, and ears respectively. For a species of insects that have inhabited our planet for almost 300 million years, it is only natural perhaps that they have such a wide and varied perception amongst various civilizations.

There are a wide variety of myths and mythology associated with the life and the existence of the dragonfly. In many regions and as a norm of this day, the dragonfly is considered to be an agent of change and presumably symbolic of a sense of self-realization.

The Hopi and their ancestors have always venerated the dragonfly. They often asked the dragonfly to confer benefits on their people. Dragonflies are portrayed on altars, pottery, and petroglyphs because the Hopi believe that dragonflies have great supernatural powers and are shamanistic. They are positive symbols of water, fertility and abundance. The Hopi people actually credit dragonflies with saving their tribe from starvation by using their supernatural powers to grow corn to maturity in four days, at the ancient time when their tribe was migrating in search of their permanent home. Similarly, butterflies undergo complete metamorphosis, passing from a larva or caterpillar stage to an immobile pupa or chrysalis, from which the winged adult emerges. Anyone observing these life stages would make the association with rebirth, resurrection, immortality and longevity, as had Chinese and Mycenaean Greeks.

Butterfly motifs can be found in Mycenaean and Hellenistic adornment. Egyptians incorporated the butterfly in their jewellery but the symbolism is not known. In addition, the butterfly stands for the soul among Greek and some pre-Hispanic cultures. Mexican colonial period art contains butterfly images likewise the Navajo and Hopi. Butterfly imagery is rampant in Chinese adornment, jewellery and clothing, as well as utilitarian objects.

In Japan the butterfly was at one time considered to be the soul of a living man or woman. If it entered a guest-room and pitched behind the bamboo screen it was a sure sign that the person whom it represented would shortly appear in the house. The presence of a butterfly in the house was regarded as a good omen, though of course everything depended on the individual typified by the butterfly. Butterflies may also be the souls of the dead, and they often appear in this form in order to announce their final leave-taking from the body.

The butterfly is the archetype of metamorphosis- the profoundest sort of physical change- and the inescapable symbol of resurrection, as the worm-like caterpillar, a creature of the earth, transforms in its quiescent pupa stage and emerges from this still and death-like state as a gaudy, gossamer creature of the air...the developmental cycle of the butterfly occurs in four stages. egg, larva or caterpillar, pupa and adult (also called imago). The metamorphosis of lepidopterans (butterflies and moths) is profoundly striking, with the obvious intimations of immortality. So it is not surprising that the human spirit or soul assumes the form of a butterfly in many myths across the world.

The butterfly was an attribute of Xochipilli, the ancient Mexican Lord of flowers and plants. Its fluttering motion suggested the flicker of firelight. And the goddess of Itzpapàlotl was portrayed as a butterfly surrounded by stone knives. She was a night spirit associated with the stars, and a symbol of the souls of women who had died in childbirth.

In Christian symbolism, this insect's metamorphosis represents the earthbound body of Jesus transformed into the luminous transcendent entity rising from the tomb.

The Angel of Death was represented by Gnostics as a winged foot crushing a butterfly, from which we may deduce that the butterfly was equated with life rather than with the soul in the sense of the spirit or transcendent being. This also explains why psychoanalysis regards the butterfly as a symbol of rebirth.

An ancient Native American legend says:

"If anyone desires a wish to come true they must capture a butterfly and whisper that wish to it. Since they make no sound, they can't tell the wish to anyone but the Great Spirit. So by making the wish and releasing the butterfly it will be taken to the heavens and be granted."

Mayans called the Hunab Ku symbol "The Galactic Butterfly" which is said to represent all of the consciousness that has ever existed in this galaxy. Elders many times interpret the arrival of the Blue Morpho butterfly as the spirit of the forest giving confirmation to a tough.

Maya Nahual: Tz'ikin

The protector, the catalyst of transformation. In dreams can reveal precious information and clarify doubts.

CROW (Raven)

Life magic

Mystery of creation

Destiny and Alchemy

Intelligence

Higher perspective

Flexibility, adaptability

Trickster, manipulative

"One for sorrow, two for mirth,

Three for a wedding, four for a birth,

Five for silver, six for gold,

Seven for a secret not to be told.

Eight for heaven, nine for hell,

And ten for the devil's own sell'."

Folk Counting Rhymes

Ravens and Crows are perhaps the most common bird symbol in the mythologies and religions of ancient cultures. They assume a variety of roles, ranging from messengers of deities and sages to oracles and tricksters. They play a central part in many creation myths and are typically associated with the supernatural realms lying beyond the ordinary experience. Studying the folk lore of different cultures may unravel the motives underlying the superstitious beliefs and religious faiths.

In most North European mythologies birds such as ravens, vultures and crows commonly pass as symbols of war, death and misfortune. Celtic and Irish goddesses were believed to appear in the form of a crow or a raven, gathering over the battlefields, where they would feed on the flesh of the fallen warriors. Also, seeing a raven or a crow before going into a battle gave a sense of foreboding and meant that the army would be defeated. When the giant Bran, king of Britain in Welsh mythology, was mortally wounded while warring against the Irish, he commanded his followers to behead him and carry his head to the Tower of London for his burial and as a sign of protection of Britain. A popular superstition arose declaring that if the ravens ever fled the Tower of London, the monarchy would fall. As long as they nested there, Britain would never be successfully invaded. In medieval times these pagan legends resulted in demonization of crows and ravens, which were consequently depicted as familiars of witches.

The history of ravens as mythical birds can be traced as far as the 1000-year-old Norse mythology. Myths describe this bird as a common sign of evil due to its habits of a scavenger. However, raven as a symbol acquires also a positive interpretation. The omniscient god Odin, one of the chief gods in Norse mythology, had a pair ravens called Hugin (Thought) and Munin (Mind) perching on his shoulders. Each daybreak they were sent out into the world to observe what was happening and question everybody, even the dead. By sunrise they would come back to whisper their master what they had seen and learnt. Since they embodied Odin's mind and thoughts, they symbolized his ability to see into the future. The book also makes a mention of an early Norse poem in which Odin sends the ravens to the Underworld to investigate the disappearance of the lost goddess Idunn.

In North American folklore ravens are the creators of the world. Details of the creation tale differ, but essentially "the Raven"—a creature with human body and raven's beak—is believed to have made the world. He gave light to people, taught them to take care of themselves, make clothes, canoes and houses. He also brought vegetation, animals, and other benefits for the human kind. Raven assumes the role of Noah from the biblical story of Great Flood—he is said to have taken animals two by two on a big raft in order to save them. After all he had done for the humans, he wished to marry a woman in turn, but her family refused to let her go. As a revenge, the myth says, the Raven created mosquitoes from crushed leaves to pester the humans forever.

The belief in intelligence and cunning of ravens or crows is unquestionable and stories paying a tribute to this "winged wisdom" may be found both in European and North American mythologies. A fable about the crow's cunning usually attributed to Aesop "The Crow and the Pitcher" is just one of the countless instances. It tells about a thirsty crow that was vainly looking for something to drink on a deserted land. When it came upon a pitcher, it found out its beak was too short to reach the water in it. It knew that if it had tipped the pitcher over, the water would spill. It dawned on it to throw pebbles in the pitcher until the water rose and reached the top. The moral arising from the fable "Necessity is the mother of invention," depicts crows as intelligent and ingenious beings.

Among the native tribes of the New World the raven is depicted both as a sage and as a trickster. Of particular interest is the story of how there was no light in the world. Though there are certain variations, the story is the same: light was kept in a box by the chief of Heaven and people lived in darkness. The raven didn't like it and conceived a plan to steal it. It took a shape of a leaf floating in a stream where the chief's daughter came to drink. She then gave birth to him and as an infant the raven played in the house of the chief. He soon began to cry for the box with the light, and the chief, charmed by his little grandson, gave it to him. The Raven changed into his bird shape and carried the box through the sky. However, he dropped it, and the light broke into tiny fragments giving rise to the stars, the moon, and the sun. In the North American mythology raven is a personification of Supreme Being. When it flaps its wings, it creates the wind, the lightning and the thunder. And it is also the raven who is responsible for the rhythm of seasons and providing the shamans with their visionary and healing powers.

North American and Canadian mythology abound in stories depicting the raven as a rascal or a trickster. Apart from the creation raven is believed to have changed the world afterwards to a less "cushy" place so that the life for humans would not be so easy. Watching humans struggle with its complexities and strenuous lots the fate dealt them was supposed to be a source of amusement for the raven.

Speaking of European cultures and Christian religion, over the centuries ravens have become symbols of something ungodly, having an evil repute. In Shakespeare's play Macbeth the ominous atmosphere is pierced by the raven's croak foreboding "the fatal entrance of Duncan." In Othello the raven flies" over the infected house." Both of these quotes have clear evil connotations.

In Alaska killing a raven was an ultimate taboo bringing on the assailant nothing less than harm. Various cases of worship might readily attest to an honoured position of ravens amounting to that of a supreme entity.

According to a Ukrainian legend the raven is believed to have had beautifully coloured feathers and a lovely voice before the Fall of Angels from heaven after which their plumage turned black and they lost their voices. It is also believed that their former beauty will be returned to them after the Paradise is restored on Earth.

An ancient American legend says: "In the olden days, the raven and the peacock were close friends who lived on a plantation. One day, the two birds decided to amuse themselves by painting each other's feathers. The raven set willingly to work and so surpassed itself that the peacock became, as it is today, one of the most beautiful birds on earth. Unwillingly to share its glory even with its friend, the mean-spirited peacock painted the raven plain black."

Popular folk superstitions myths are based on the belief that when someone dies, his/her soul goes to the land of the dead, in Celtic known as "Otherworld" or in some parts of Africa as "Underworld". If someone died earlier then he/she was supposed to, they would come back after death to complete their interrupted fate, the murdered would return for revenge, and those who were not buried in holy grounds would return to have their coffins moved to a more peaceful place. Dead people would return as animals. E.A. Poe's "The Raven" may serve as an illustration of this folkloristic tradition. In E.A. Poe's poem, the narrator asks the Raven, which had flown into his chamber, whether he will ever be reunited with his beloved deceased, but the Raven only gazes placidly as befits a messenger from the world beyond.

While for Christians raven symbolizes the evil opposite of the innocent dove, in most of the North American traditions raven is seen as the mediator between the land of the living and the land of the dead, accompanying the dead souls on their final journey. Indian tribes in the American Southwest, worshippers of the Ghost Dance religion engaged in an ecstatic dance to bring about the regeneration of the earth. They would decorate themselves with crow feathers, paint crows on their clothes and sing to the crow. Sometimes they would sing of their shaman, Wowoka, flying around the world in the form of a crow.

As a spirit guide, the crow will guide you in getting in touch with life mysteries and develop your ability to perceive subtle shifts in energy within yourself and in your environment. It has the ability to go beyond the illusions, especially duality of right and wrong, inner and outer.

Mayan people connect the crow with death, even if it recalls the duty on earth.

Maya Nahual: Ajmaq

The Vulture, representing all the sinners and the braves.

OWL

Intuition, ability to see beyond deceit and masks

Profound wisdom

Transition and insight

Sacred Medicine

Life beyond death

"Eyes of night, silent fliers through dark skies

Lend me your vision that I might find my way to secret knowledge

Teach me to listen that I might hear wisdom

when it moves in the world

Unite my heart and my mind

and let me feel your wings opening in my life"

Owl Prayer – Travis Bowman

Throughout history and across many cultures, people have regarded Owls with fascination and awe. Few other creatures have so many different and contradictory beliefs about them. Owls have been feared and venerated, despised and admired, considered wise and foolish, and associated with witchcraft and medicine, the weather, birth and death.

In early Indian folklore, owls represent wisdom and helpfulness, and have powers of prophecy. This theme recurs in Aesop's fables and in Greek myths and beliefs. By the Mid Ages in Europe, the owl had become the associate of witches and the inhabitant of dark, lonely and profane places, a foolish but feared spectre. An owl's appearance at night, when people are helpless and blind, linked them with the unknown, its eerie call filled people with foreboding and apprehension: a death was imminent or some evil was at hand. During the eighteenth century the zoological aspects of owls were detailed through close observation, reducing the mystery surrounding these birds. With superstitions dying out in the twentieth century - in the West at least - the owl has returned to its position as a symbol of wisdom.

In the mythology of ancient Greece, Athena, the Goddess of Wisdom, was so impressed by the great eyes and solemn appearance of the owl that, having banished the mischievous crow, she honoured the night bird by making him her favourite among feathered creatures. This owl was protected and inhabited the acropolis in great numbers. It was believed that a magical inner light gave owl night vision. As the symbol of Athena, the owl was a protector, accompanying Greek armies to war, and providing ornamental inspiration for their daily lives. If an owl flew over Greek soldiers before a battle, they took it as a sign of victory. The little owl also kept a watchful eye on Athenian trade and commerce from the reverse side of their coins.

According to Artemidorus, a second Century soothsayer, to dream of an Owl meant that a traveller would be shipwrecked or robbed.

In Roman Mythology, Persephone was transported to the underworld against her will by Hades, god of the underworld, and was to be allowed to return to her mother Demeter, goddess of agriculture, providing she ate nothing while in the underworld. Ascalpus, however, saw her picking a pomegranate, and told what he had seen. He was turned into an owl for his sin - "a sluggish Screech Owl, a loathsome bird."

The traditional shamanic meaning of the owl spirit animal is the announcer of death, most likely symbolic like a life transition, change. It is considered a very feminine force, associated with the moon and lunar energy. It is often linked to people who have psychic or medium abilities. Among some native groups in the Pacific Northwest of USA, owls served to bring shamans in contact with the dead, provided power for seeing at night, or gave power that enabled a shaman to find lost objects.

Old-forest owls, particularly the Forest Eagle-owl, play major roles in many Nepali and Hindu legends. As heard calling at night from cemeteries and sacred groves, such owls are thought to have captured the spirit of a person departed from this world. In China, owlets have been believed to pluck out their mothers' eyes and the owl's night excursions have led to a wide-spread association with occult powers. The bird's superb night vision may underlie its connection with prophecy, and the reputation for being all-seeing could arise from its ability to turn its head through almost 180 degrees.

The owl holds a special place in the Cherokee creation myth. According to legend: "earth as a floating island began from nothing but water, with all the animals living in an upper world known as Galunlati. When Galunlati became crowded, the water beetle ventured below and made islands from the mud under the water. The Great Buzzard, father of all buzzards on Earth, then came and formed valleys and mountains with the flapping of his wings. Although the Cherokee do not claim to know who made the plants and animals that came to inhabit the Earth, it is thought the animals from the upper world were told to keep watch over these newly created creatures for seven nights. Only the owl and the cougar endured this seven-day stretch, which is why they have the power to see in the dark." The Mayans called the screech owl of the Yucatan "the moan bird," and believed that it meant death. Ah Puch, Maya god of death, also known as Hunhau, ruled over Mitnal, the land of death, the lowest and worst of the nine hells. He was normally shown with the head of an owl on a human body. To this day, the Indians of Central America and Mexico believe that someone will die when the owl screeches. For contemporary Maya shamans, the owl is the manifestation of obscurity, of the unknown and of magic. They associate the night creature to the hidden power to heal a person close to death by using sacred medicine and secret knowledge.

Maya Nahual: Kame

The death guardian is the source of wisdom and everlasting protection. The owl in dreams can stimulate the intuition and the desire for exploring the magic realm.

BEE

Prophecy
Productivity and Fertility
Sun Energy
Resolution
Loving and Caring

"How doth the little busy bee

improve each shining hour,

and gather honey all the day

from every opening flower."

Isaac Watts

Bees have been worshipped and assumed to have prophetic powers since ancient times.

The worldwide prevalence of bee myths and veneration for bees suggests possibilities including very early interaction and veneration of bees, or that bees represent a Jungian archetype.

In Ancient India and Ancient Greece lips anointed with honey have been associated with eloquence and even prescience, while the bee colony has often been taken as a model of society.

The bee is also sometimes a symbol of immortality and resurrection and more often of industriousness.

In ancient Egypt bees were regarded as the tears of the Sun god Ra while some consider the Fleur de Lys as derived not from the lily but as a stylised representation of the bees associated with the goddess Artemis.

In Finland the Kalevala tells how a mother implored the bee Mehilainen to fly three times to gather honey to bring her dead son Lemminkainen back to life. On the third flight the bee brought honey back from heaven and when spread on the son's body the son came back to life. The son's death and resurrection have a parallel in the death and resurrection of Osiris. The son was killed and cut into eight pieces after an unsuccessful trip courting and his mother reassembled all the pieces. Similarly Osiris was killed by Set who cut the body into 14 parts and scattered them. Isis gathered 13 of the parts and eventually resurrected Osiris. Similarly in some shamanic initiations the new shaman is torn to pieces by spirits and put together again. Some modern shamans experience the same thing, in one case having some bees extracted from inside them.

The same epic describes the mythical origin of the bee as created when a young girl, Osmotar, who had failed to get ale of barley and hops to ferment, picked up a pea plant and rolled it in her hands and with her thighs till a bee was born. She then instructed the bee to fetch honey and the honey started the fermentation.

In the Greek Homeric Hymn to Hermes written down in the eighth century BC, the god Apollo talks of three female seers as three bees or bee-maidens, who like himself, practiced divination. These sacred bee-maidens with their gift of prophecy, who sometimes told truth and sometimes lies, were Apollo's gift to Hermes who had first tricked Apollo out of his cattle then charmed Apollo into giving him the cattle.

There are certain holy ones, sisters born

three virgins gifted with wings:

their heads are besprinkled with white meal, and they dwell under a ridge of Parnassos.

These are teachers of divination apart from me,

the art which I practised while yet a boy following herds,

though my father paid no heed to it.

From their home they fly now here, now there,

feeding on honey-comb and bringing all things to pass.

And when they are inspired through eating yellow honey, they are willing to speak the truth;

but if they be deprived of the gods' sweet food,

then they speak falsely, as they swarm in and out together.

Apollo did not however give everything to Hermes, the Oracle at Delphi was known as the Delphic Bee and it seems one of the Thriae was named Daphnis (Laurel) after the laurel leave used to create her intoxicated prophetic trance.

The bee maidens were usually identified with the Thriae, a trinity of pre-Hellenic Aegean bee goddesses, also identified and three prophetic nymphs on Mount Parnassus, by whom Apollo was reared, and who were believed to have invented the art of prophecy by means of little stones (thriai), which were thrown into an urn. They are examples of a trinity that crops up in many places: the Maiden, Matron and crone of Wicca, the three Norns, the three furies, the three witches in the Scottish play, and the Three Fates.

The Eleusinian Mysteries were an initiatory tradition in Greece that played an important role in the lives of those who experienced it. In these rites, the initiates, known as mystai, were led on a procession toward Eleusis by the priests and priestesses of Demeter. This was a symbolic journey in which they purified themselves in preparation to ceremonially return Persephone from the underworld and take part in other sacred acts. As in the wider Greek culture, the bee symbolized divine concepts of life and death, so in the Mysteries and other traditions it took on the connotation of death and rebirth: that is, of personal regeneration and transformation.

Also, Dionysus was said to have made the first hives and showed his people how to gather honey.

As the legend goes: Melissa (meaning bee) cared for the infant Zeus while he was being hidden from his father, Chronos, the king of all the gods. Melissa fed Zeus a diet of stolen honey. When discovered, she was turned into a lowly form of an insect. Bees were considered a higher form of an insect and Zeus knew she kept him alive, so he turned her into a bee.

The Bee Totem is a universal symbol of diligence obedience and the work ethic. Many cultures see the bee as the messengers of the Gods and a symbol of the human soul.

Native American Indians believe that bees represent immortality and selflessness.

The Royal Bee Totem possesses the following virtues: messages from higher planes and consciousness, prophetic dreams and visions, industry, wealth, industriousness, diligence, cooperation, productive hard work, sexual attraction, the power of giving back when taking, the ability to turn something unassuming into a wonderful creation, ability to enjoy and savour the sweetness of life, connection with the earth and living things, divine messages, productiveness, focus, sensitivity, and realizing the fruit of one's labour.

The Mayan deity, Muzen Cab, was The Great Guardian of Honey or the great Lord of Bees. There was also a Bee God, Mok Chi, who could transform into Bees. The Mayan apiculture is very spiritual and complex and was strongly related to the days of the calendar, as explained in the Madrid Codex.

The beehives in Mayan culture were positioned towards the four cardinal points that hold the universe. Each cardinal point or "Bacab" had its importance. For example the eastern Bacab was in the direction they believed was where honey was produced.

According to ancient Mayan myths, the first inhabitants; called Zayawinicoub, ate up all the royal honey they were harvesting. To avoid facing death as punishment from their gods, Hobin (god of the beehive) turned them into stingless bees so they could restock the honey.

Maya Nahual: Ajmak

It represents forgiveness and resolution.

JAGUAR (Leopard, Puma, Panther)

Strength and Fertility

Supreme focus

Visualization and Manifestation

Shamanism

Spiritual breathe

Shapeshifting and Prophecy

"Spread the jaguar's skin,

and you spread the heavens of a starry night."

Mayan saying

The Jaguar is part of a long history in the lore and mythology of several indigenous cultures. In particular, the Mayans held the Jaguar in high esteem, viewing this spotted panther as the Totem Spirit of the Sky God.

It is said that a Great Being came to the Mayan people from the stars, and taught them that the greatest of all virtues was integrity. He instructed the people in the beauty of unconditional love, forgiveness, peace and to be honourable and trustworthy. The teachings were of the sacrificial heart, the willingness to give freely of one's self and one's material belongings in order to benefit both the individual and the collective All. Generations later, it is believed that the sacrificial heart became literal as a bloody sacrifice wherein the heart of the victim would be taken from the body and given to the Jaguar Spirit in the hopes of appeasing the Sky God.

The sacrifices had the opposite of their desired effect and, instead of pleasing the Sky God, angered him. To instruct the people that such ways were not a part of his teaching, the Sky God then sent the Jaguar Spirit to prowl the dreams of the two-legged people. Where the Jaguar found hearts blackened with hatred, greed or dishonesty, he would haunt those unfortunate souls, relentlessly stalking them until they embraced the wisdom of integrity and transformed their lives. Those who resisted were met with the vengeance of the jaguar, and the Animal Totem's relentless pursuit during the dreamtime would often cause the human to transition from fright. For the two-legged beside whom jaguar walks, the path will be a process of reconnecting to the shaman within.

The Jaguar individual it is said to be a wide-open vessel through which great mystery may flow. This soul will hear, see or feel things that are non-physical in nature.

According to one Maya myth, it was a supernatural being, Jaguar Sun, who rose each day in the east and prowled west, aging along the course, until finally plunging into the darkness of the west. Then Jaguar Sun fights the Lords of Xibalba (the Underworld) all night. Through his strength and cunning, Jaguar Sun wins the right to rise each day in the East. Thus Jaguar Sun dominates both day and night.

We can sum up the general jaguar archetype by saying he is a deadly and immensely effective warrior. The jaguar shaman because of his strength is able to "dominate the spirits, in the same way as a predator dominates its prey".

Similarly, the panther archetype is a symbol of unleashing desires, and thus the awakening of passion. It symbolize a time of moving from mere poles of existence to new life without poles or barriers. The panther is also a symbol associated with Bacchus/Dionysus. One story tells how Bacchus was nursed by panthers, and he is sometimes depicted riding a chariot drawn by them. The myths and stories of Dionysus are very symbolic. The panther in a Dionysic manner awakens the unconscious urges and abilities that have been closed down. It signals a time of imminent awakening.

The panther is a symbol of awakening to the heroic quest. All of the Greek heroes were born from the union of a god and a mortal mother, the linking of the great fire and the great femininity. The heroes thus had the seeds of the divine force, which would eventually provide impetus to reach beyond the normal bounds and restrictions, to negotiate new stages in progression and purification. The heroic tales tell that no matter the depth of degradation, there is always the promise of light and love to lead us back. When the panther enters your life, the path leading back is about to begin.

To the Indians of North and South America, the panther was endowed with great magic and power. The jaguar panther climbs, runs, and swims-- even better than the tiger. Because it could function so well in so many areas, it became a symbol of immeasurable power to the Latin American natives. It was a symbol of mastery over all dimensions.

To the Tucano Indians of the Amazon, the roar of the jaguar was the roar of thunder. Thus the panther was the god of darkness and could cause eclipses by swallowing the sun. This reflects the tremendous power inherent within the feminine forces.

The Arawak Indians say that everything has jaguar. Nothing exists without it. It is the tie to all life and all manifestations of life. To them, becoming the man-jaguar was the ultimate shapeshifting ritual.

Even in Egyptian rituals, a panther tail was worn about the waist or knotted about the neck to help protect and strengthen. It was used in a process called "passage through the skin", their own version of shapeshifting to engender themselves with the panther's power.

Maya Nahual: Ix

Strength and power, the primordial, essential being and the powerful shaman. In dreams it recalls the sense of grounding and the necessity to follow a spiritual path, instead of fighting and struggling. The Jaguar can be seen as a great manifestation of a tribe leader vocation.

SNAKE

Healing
Transformation
Primal Force
Creation
Underworld

"..and you can see her, you can see the Benevolent Rainbow Serpent

as she travels from one waterhole to another

as she emerges from one and she is in the sky

and you can see her

the lovely creative Rainbow Serpent in the sky

and she disappears soon enough

into another huge waterhole

somewhere on our earth

the rainbow snake

see it tickles, the frogs

and water fills the rivers and gullies and waterholes;

and see the rainbow snake

see it brings forth all life sleeping before"

Aboriginal Poem

Serpents and snakes play a role in many of the world's myths and legends. Sometimes these mythic beasts appear as ordinary snakes. At other times, they take on magical or monstrous forms. Serpents and snakes have long been associated with good as well as with evil, representing life and death, creation and destruction.

In religion, mythology, and literature, serpents and snakes often stand for fertility or a creative life force—partly because the creatures can be seen as symbols of the male sex organ. They have also been associated with water and earth because many kinds of snakes live in the water or in holes in the ground.

In Judeo-Christian tradition the snake in the Garden of Eden story is connected to sin, whereas for many other cultures snakes and serpents are associated with healing and regeneration.

The ancient Chinese connected serpents with life-giving rain. Traditional beliefs in Australia, India, North America, and Africa have linked snakes with rainbows, which in turn are often related to rain and fertility. The Aboriginal Australian Rainbow Serpent meanders like a snaking river across the landscape, sunlight reflecting the spectrum of colours. He inhabits permanent waterholes and controls precious oils and waters. Unpredictable, he vies with the ever-burning Sun, replenishing stores of water, forming gullies and deep channels as he slithers across the land, collecting and distributing the rivers of life.

Dreamtime stories tell of the great spirits and totems during creation, in animal and human form they moulded the barren and featureless earth. The Rainbow Serpent came from beneath the ground and created huge ridges, mountains and gorges as it pushed upward. The Rainbow Serpent is known as Ngalyod by the Gunwinggu and Borlung by the Miali. He is a serpent of immense proportions which inhabits deep permanent waterholes. Descended from that larger being visible as a dark streak in the Milky Way, it reveals itself to people in this world as a rainbow as it moves through water and rain, shaping landscapes, naming and singing of places, swallowing and sometimes drowning people; strengthening the knowledgeable with rainmaking and healing powers; blighting others with sores, weakness, illness, and death.

The ancient Greeks considered snakes sacred to Asclepius, the god of medicine. He carried a caduceus, a staff with one or two serpents wrapped around it, which has become the symbol of modern physicians.

For both the Greeks and the Egyptians, the snake represented eternity. Ouroboros, the Greek symbol of eternity, consisted of a snake curled into a circle or hoop, biting its own tail. The Ouroboros grew out of the belief that serpents eat themselves and are reborn from themselves in an endless cycle of destruction and creation. The Ouroboros symbol in Alchemy, was also seen as a symbol of assimilation. Consumption of the opposites. This sign was also regarded as a symbol for immortality as the serpent never dies and is always reborn.

The snake is seen as a sacred creature in Africa, especially in West Africa. The Ouroboros symbol is prevalent in many religious aspects in the form of the Oshunmare. The Oshunmare is also seen as a symbol for rebirth.

The Nagas of Hindu and Buddhist mythology show how serpents can symbolize both good and evil, hopes and fears. Although these snake gods could take any shape, including a fully human one, they often appeared as human heads on serpent bodies. The Nagas lived in underwater or underground kingdoms. They controlled rainfall and interacted with deities and humans in a variety of ways. Some were good, such as Muchalinda, the snake king who shielded Buddha from a storm. Others could be cruel and vengeful.

In Toltec and Aztec mythology, Quetzalcoatl, the Feathered Serpent, held an important place. The Maya version of Quetzalcoatl is Kukulcan, one of the three gods that was thought to have created the earth. The legend says that he came from heaven to earth, and because of that he was represented as a feathered serpent in all the ruins of Mexico's archaeological sites. Half man and half god in one same being.

The quetzal bird representing heaven and the serpent representing earth. White-skinned and bearded, Kukulkan was also the god of life and divine wisdom. He brought love, penitence, and exemption from the usual rituals of sacrifice and blood offering. He was a mystical man who met with people from distant places, and had the power to heal the sick and bring the dead back to life. When he departed for the east, travelling the ocean on a raft of serpents, he promised his followers that he would return.

In medieval Europe, people told tales of the basilisk, a serpent with a dragon's body that could kill merely by looking at or breathing on its victims. Melusina, another figure in European folklore, was part woman, part fish and snake and had to spend one day each week in water.

In the mythology of ancient Egypt, Apopis was a demon of chaos who appeared in the form of a serpent. Each night he attacked Ra, the sun god. But Mehen, another huge serpent, coiled himself around Ra's sun boat to protect the god from Apopis—a perfect illustration of how snakes can be symbols of both good and evil in mythology.

Mythological snakes that act as forces of good have various roles, such as creating the world, protecting it, or helping humans. Stories of the Fon people of West Africa tell of Da, a serpent whose 3,500 coils support the cosmic ocean in which the earth floats. Another 3,500 of its coils support the sky. Humans occasionally catch a glimpse of many-coloured Da in a rainbow or in light reflected on the surface of water.

According to a story of the Diegueño Indians of California, humans obtained many of the secrets of civilization from a huge serpent named Umai-hulhlya-wit. This serpent lived in the ocean until people performed a ceremony and called him onto the land. They built an enclosure for him, but it was too small to hold him. After Umai-hulhlya-wit had squeezed as much of himself as possible into the enclosure, the people set him on fire. Soon the serpent's body exploded, showering the earth with the knowledge, secrets, songs, and other cultural treasures he had contained.

Hindu myths contain many tales of serpents. Kaliya was a five-headed serpent king who poisoned water and land until the god Krishna defeated him in battle. Kaliya then worshiped Krishna, who spared his life. Kadru was a snake goddess who bore 1,000 children. Legend says that they still live today as snakes in human form. One of Kadru's children was the world snake Shesha that the gods used to turn a mountain and stir up the ocean, just as people churn milk into butter by using a rope coiled around a stick or paddle. As the gods churned the ocean with the snake, many precious things arose from it, including the moon, a magical tree, and the Amrita, or water of life.

In terms of Jungian psychology, snake dreams have a powerful archetypal quality. They give people an extremely memorable and uncanny experience of the "otherness" of the collective unconscious.

"The serpent is an adversary and a symbol of enmity, but also a wise bridge that connects right and left through longing, much needed by our life." Carl Jung said.

Maya Nahual: Kan

The Kan Nahual energy corresponds to the energy of the Kundalini, a concept shared by Mayans and Hindus. This is the sexual fire energy that is dormant in our first chakra and moving up our spine uncovering and healing our body, is the energy which deals with adequate and balanced management of sexuality, in discovering the magic and joy of life.

SPIDER

Feminine Energy
Creativity
Shadow Self
Life Connections and Destiny
Universal Laws

"Corn spider woman marches up the red mountain in the dark moon

where the sun has set to sing with a feather

which has been sitting upon the skin of a drum

carrying the hearts of the women

the ones who are here now

she will sit singing, she will sent riibering

while the old man makes the evening"

Tobacco Indigenous Song

The spider is an ancient and powerful symbol found around the globe, and has always elicited a wide range of emotions in people: fear, disgust, panic, and sometimes curiosity and appreciation. This broad spectrum of impressions has influenced origin myths, legends, art, literature, music, architecture, and technology throughout history.

Arachnids and their webs embody many traits and interpretations, including resourcefulness, creation and destruction, cunning, deception, intrigue, the feminine, wisdom, fortune, patience, and death.

In one ancient Greek legend, the world's first spider was born from the pride of a woman. The mortal Arachne was gifted in the art of weaving fine cloth and tapestries, and studied under the goddess Athena, herself a master at weaving and pottery. Arachne's work was so beautiful, and her talent so great, that word of her weaving spread far and wide. Eventually, pride and arrogance lead Arachne to boast that her work was even better than Athena's. In a contest to determine who was the better artist – the mortal or the goddess - Arachne wove a tapestry depicting the gods in a bad light, detailing their debauchery and foolishness. The goddess Athena was furious and, in a rage, destroyed Arachne's work.

Arachne, horrified and ashamed to realize where her hubris had taken her, hanged herself. Athena, feeling that the mortal had learned the error of challenging the gods, turned the hanging rope into web, and Arachne into a spider, so she might weave beautiful creations for all time. This is the origin of the word arachnid, a term we use for spiders to this day.

Spider Woman appears in the mythology of several Native American tribes, including the Navajo, Keresan, and Hopi. In most cases, she is associated with the emergence of life on earth. She helps humans by teaching them survival skills. Spider Woman also teaches the Navajos the art of weaving. Before weavers sit down at the loom, they often rub their hands in spider webs to absorb the wisdom and skill of Spider Woman.

In the Navajo creation story, Spider Woman (Na'ashjéii asdzáá) helps the warrior twins Monster Slayer and Child of Water find their father, the Sun. The Keresan say that Spider Woman gave the corn goddess Iyatiku a basket of seeds to plant.

According to the Hopi, at the beginning of time Spider Woman controlled the underworld, the home of the gods, while the sun god Tawa ruled the sky. Using only their thoughts, they created the earth between the two other worlds. Spider Woman moulded animals from clay, but they remained lifeless. So she and Tawa spread a soft white blanket over them, said some magic words, and the creatures began to move. Spider Woman then moulded people from clay. To bring them to life, she clutched them to her breast and, together with Tawa, sang a song that made them into living beings. She divided the animals and people into the groups that inhabit the earth today. She also gave men and women specific roles: Women were to watch over the home and men to pray and make offerings to the gods.

In ancient India, it is written that a large spider wove the web that is our universe. She sits at the centre of the web, controlling everything with her strings. The legend said that she will one day devour the web/universe, and spin another in its place.

Egyptian mythology tells of the goddess Neith - a spinner and weaver of destiny - and associates her with the spider. She is often depicted with a weaving shuttle in her hand, or a bow and arrows, demonstrating her hunting abilities.

The spider is a trickster god in West African stories, personifying the creation deity Anansi. Associated with storytelling and wisdom, the spider causes mischief to get the upper hand in dealings with others. The retelling of these "spider tales" imparts moral lessons through the generations.

Rock art and bark paintings in Australia reveal that the indigenous cultures created spider symbols. Spiders in their webs are linked with a sacred rock and ceremony for the Rembarrnga people in central Arnhem Land. Several regional clans use spider totems in rituals.

Ancient Chinese folk culture celebrates spiders. They are thought to bring happiness to the morning, and wealth in the evening.

"In several cultures, spiders are credited with saving the lives of great leaders. In the Torah, there is a story of David, who would later become King of Israel, being pursued by soldiers sent by King Saul. David hid in a cave, and a spider crawled in and built a huge web across the entrance. When the soldiers saw the cave, they didn't bother to search it – after all, no one could be hiding inside it if the spider web was undisturbed. A parallel story appears in the life of the prophet Mohammed, who hid in a cave when fleeing his enemies. A giant tree sprouted in front of the cave, and a spider built a web between the cave and the tree, with similar results." Mythologist Patti Wigington, said.

The mysterious Nazca lines in the desert of southern Peru contain arachnid imagery. The series of geoglyphs depict straight lines and giant creatures, and were created between 400 and 650 AD. The largest image spans over 200 meters across. One of the geoglyph creatures is a giant, symmetrical, eight-legged spider. Some suggest the spider could have been a fertility symbol in the Nazca culture, and the senior astronomer at the Adler Planetarium and Astronomy Museum posits that the spider is a representation of the Orion constellation.

The Mayans recognized the mystic spider that weaves intergalactic threads, the conduit of interconnected consciousness. Yellow Warrior is the spider in the web, the grid connection for divine communication.

The Teotihuacan Spider Woman was a goddess of the Pre-Columbian Teotihuacan civilization, Maya, in what is now Mexico. The great goddess wears a frame headdress that often includes the face of a jaguar and has a medallion in the centre on which an owl is usually depicted.

She will also be shown among several spiders and is frequently seen with a yellow body coloration, further distinguishing her from other Mesoamerican deities. This Spider Woman is now thought to have been a goddess of the underworld, darkness, the earth, water, war, and possibly even creation itself.

Maya Nahual: Kat

The spider represents the network of possibilities and life connections. She guides the dreamer in weaving his destiny.

DOG

Loyalty
Offering and Devotion
Guardian of the Underworld
Virtue and Vice
Fear and Destruction

"'This sweet to hear the watch dog's honest bark

Bay deep-mouthed welcome as we draw near home;

'tis sweet to know there is an eye will mark

Our coming and look brighter when we come."

Lord Byron

Dogs have been a part of the history of human beings since before the written word. In many cultures throughout the ancient world, dogs figured prominently and, largely, were regarded in much the same way that they are today. Dogs were seen as faithful companions, hunters, guardians, and as a treasured part of the family.

In the oldest story from the Near East, The Epic of Gilgamesh from ancient Mesopotamia (dated to 2150-1400 BCE), dogs appear in an elevated role as the companions of one of the most popular goddesses of the region; the goddess Innana (Ishtar) travels with seven prized hunting dogs. In the famous Descent of Innana (a story considered older than and not a part of Gilgamesh) in which the goddess goes down into the underworld, her husband, Dumuzi, keeps domesticated dogs as part of his royal retinue. Dogs featured prominently in the everyday life of the Mesopotamians.

The dog connection with the gods and the dog's loyalty to human beings is further explored in other cultures. In ancient Egypt the dog was linked to the jackal god, Anubis, who guided the soul of the deceased to the Hall of Truth where the soul would be judged by the great god Osiris. Domesticated dogs were buried with great ceremony in the temple of Anubis at Saqqara and the idea behind this seemed to be to help the deceased dogs pass on easily to the afterlife (known in Egypt as the Field of Reeds) where they could continue to enjoy their lives as they had on earth. Dogs were highly valued in Egypt as part of the family and, when a dog would die, the family, if they could afford to, would have the dog mummified with as much care as they would pay for a human member of the family. Great grief was displayed over the death of a family dog and the family would shave their eyebrows as a sign of this grief (as they also did with their cats). Tomb paintings of the pharaoh Rameses the Great depict him with his hunting dogs and dogs were often buried with their masters to provide this kind of companionship in the afterlife.

In ancient India the dog was also highly regarded. The Indian Pariah Dog, which still exists today, is considered by many to be the first truly domesticated dog in history and the oldest in the world (though this has been challenged). The great cultural epic The Mahabharata (around 400 BCE) significantly features a dog who may have been one of these Pariah Dogs. The epic relates, toward the end, the tale of King Yudisthira, many years after the Battle of Kurukshetra, making a pilgrimage to his final resting place. On the way he is accompanied by his family and his faithful dog. One by one his family members die along the path but his dog remains by his side. When, at last, Yudisthira reaches the gates of paradise he is welcomed for the good and noble life he has lived but the guardian at the gate tells him the dog is not allowed inside. Yudisthira is shocked that so loyal and noble a creature as his dog would not be allowed into heaven and so chooses to remain with his dog on earth, or even go to hell, than enter into a place which would exclude the dog. The guardian at the gate then tells Yudisthira that this was only a last test of his virtue and that, of course, the dog is welcome to enter also. In some versions of this tale the dog is then revealed to be the god Vishnu, the preserver, who has been watching over Yudisthira all his life, thus linking the figure of the dog directly to the concept of god.

The dog appears in Greek literature early on in the figure of the three-headed dog Cerberus who guarded the gates of Hades. One example of this in art is the Caeretan black-figure hydria vase of Heracles and Cerberus from c. 530-520 BCE. In Greece, as in ancient Sumeria, the dog was associated with female deities in that both the goddesses Artemis and Hecate kept dogs (Artemis, hunting dogs while Hecate kept black Molossian dogs).

Dogs are also featured in Plato's famous dialogue of Republic. Socrates claims that the dog is a true philosopher because dogs "distinguish the face of a friend and of an enemy only by the criterion of knowing and not knowing" and concludes that dogs must be lovers of learning because they determine what they like and what they do not based upon knowledge of the truth.

Ancient China had an interesting relationship with the dog. Dogs were the earliest animals domesticated in China (c. 12,000 BCE) along with pigs and were used in hunting and kept as companions. They were also used, very early on, as a food source and as sacrifices. Ancient oracle bones (which were the bones of animals or shells of turtles used to tell the future) mention dogs repeatedly as both good and bad omens depending upon how, in what condition, and under what circumstances, the dog was seen. The blood of a dog was an important component in sealing oaths and swearing allegiances because dogs were thought to have been given to humans as a gift from heaven and so their blood was sacred. As a gift from the divine, they were honoured but it was understood that they had been provided for a purpose: to help human beings survive by providing them with food and with blood for sacrifice.

The Maya had a similar relationship with dogs as the Chinese. Dogs were bred in pens as a food source, as guardians and pets, and for hunting, but were also associated with the gods. As dogs were noted as great swimmers, they were thought to conduct the souls of the dead across the watery expanse to the afterlife, the netherworld of Xibalba. Once the soul had arrived in the dark realm, the dog served as a guide to help the deceased through the challenges presented by the Lords of Xibalba and to reach paradise. This has been inferred from excavations in the region which have uncovered graves in which dogs are buried with their masters and from inscriptions on temple walls. Similar inscriptions in the surviving Mayan Codices depict the dog as the bringer of fire to the people and, in the Quiche Maya holy book, the Popol Vuh, dogs are instrumental in the destruction of the ungrateful and unknowing race of humans which the gods first produced and then repented of.

The Aztecs and Tarascans shared this view of the dog, including the dog as a guide to the afterlife for the deceased. The Aztecs also had a story in their mythology regarding the destruction of an early race of human beings in which dogs are featured. In this tale, the gods drown the world in a great flood but a man and woman manage to survive by clinging to a log. Once the waters recede, they climb onto dry land and build a fire to dry themselves. The smoke from this fire annoys the great god Tezcatlipoca who tears off their heads and then sews the heads to the rear-end of the man and woman and, in doing so, creates dogs. According to this myth, dogs pre-date the present race of human beings and so should be treated with respect the way one would treat an elder. The Aztecs also buried dogs with their dead and their god of death, Xolotl, was imagined as a huge dog.

Maya Nahual: Tzi'

It may represents impurity and emotional instability. Tzi'is also the authority and the fear of revealing secrets of the shadow self.

DEER

Grace and Sensitivity

Vigilance

Ability to regenerate

The Inner Child

Innocence

"They have gone by the painted desert

where the dawn mists lie uncurled

and over the purple barrows

on the outer rim of the world

The people shout from the village

and the sun gets up to spy

the royal deer and the runner

clear shining in the sky"

The Deer Star- Indigenous poem

In many European mythologies the deer was associated with woodland deities. Two tales of Artemis, the Greek goddess of wilderness, tell of her wrath and retribution visited upon those who trespassed into her domain. By controlling the weather she kept King Agamemnon's fleet bound for Troy confined to port, to avenge the killing of a stag sacred to her. Another hunter, Acteon, used a stag's pelt to sneak up on Artemis whilst she was bathing in the forest. As punishment for seeing her naked, she changed him into a stag and sent him back into the woods to be hunted down and killed by its hounds.

Other woodland goddesses, such as Diana, the Roman equivalent of Artemis, were similarly associated with deer and their perceived qualities of gracefulness and swiftness.

In Irish mythology Finn Mac Cumhail, the legendary leader of Ireland's heroic band of warriors known as the Fianna, cornered a beautiful white deer, which his hounds then refused to dispatch. That night Finn was visited by the goddess Sadb, who explained that a spell had turned her into the deer Finn had chased, a spell from which his love could release her. Though they became lovers, the magician who cast the spell reclaimed Sadb when Finn was away repelling a Viking raid on Dublin, and though the Fianna searched the land, Sadb could not be found. Some years later however, another of Finn mac Cumhail's hunting sorties tracked down a naked, long haired boy whom once again his hounds refused to kill. The boy did not know his father but knew his mother to be a gentle hind who lived in fear of another man. Details of the story convinced Finn that this was his son, and he named him Oisin, meaning fawn.

In Celtic religion the stag was a symbol for the god Cernunnos, "The Horned One". Cernunnos was often portrayed with antlers himself, and was a god of the forest and wild animals. He was also seen as a god of 'Plenty', and the large Celtic 'Cauldrons of Plenty' often featured deer motifs amongst their ornate decoration. The magnificent Gundestrup Cauldron, for example, shows an antlered man alongside a deer and other wildlife. Though this is often regarded as a representation of Cernunnos, his pose in a half lotus position suggests he could also be a Celtic shaman.

In Native American mythology there is the Chickasaw legend, the Ghost of the White Deer symbolizing spirituality.

"This white one represents the sacredness of all living things and they should be left alone, never hunted or bothered. When we see them, we should take notice of our own spirituality and think about where we are with it."

There is also a Lenape legend about white deer that predicts that when a pair of all-white deer is seen together, it is a sign that the indigenous peoples of the Dawnland will all come together and lead the world with their wisdom.

Many tribes and indigenous peoples throughout the world have similar myths. The Seneca, Roanoke, Algonquin, Nanticoke, and Pocomoke tribes all relate sightings of the Great White Deer.

In Kamakura, Japan, the Engakuji Temple, which was founded in 1282, is the head of a branch school of the Rinzai sect of Zen Buddhism. There a herd of divine white deer are said to have emerged from a cave to listen to the sermon of the temple's founder the day it opened.

In Mexico Huichol people connect the peyote with deer. It is suggested that the Peyote Hunt represents a historical and mystical return to the original Huichol homeland and way of life, and a symbolic re-creation of "original times" before the present separation occurred between man, gods, plants, and animals; between life and death, between the natural and supernatural; and between the sexes. On the Peyote Hunt, men become gods and at the most dramatic moment of the event, when the first peyote is "slain" and eaten, the important social distinctions of age, sex, ritual status, regional differences and family affiliations, are eliminated. A state of unity and continuity, which epitomizes the Huichol view of "the good," is reached and this continuity is between man, nature, society, and the supernatural. The "retrieval" of this unity is seen as perhaps the most important function of the ceremony, and of the entire symbol complex.

Mayans respect the deer as a powerful animal and they still perform a folk dance called "baile del venado". The deer dance is a ancient custom that depicts a scene from around the time of the Spanish conquest. Participants wear masks and costumes that resemble two Europeans and several animals. The dance begins as one of the Europeans sees an animal in the forest and asks a Maya what it is. A Maya man tells him that it's a deer. The European asks if they eat deer, to which the response is no, because they don't have the tools needs to catch deer. All this is done by corporal gestures as the dancers sway back and forth to the cheerful rhythm of the marimba. The story continues as the European instructs the villager to go up to the mountain where another European lives and ask him to hunt a deer. His instructions are carried out but not before praying to Tzuultaq'a, god of the hill. The Europeans then produce a gun which is used to shoot a rabid deer at an opening near the river. At which point the rest of the animals in the forest, other deer, the monkey, the tiger and the lion then carry the hunter out of the forest so that he not continue hunting and to celebrate a successful hunt. At the end they all dance together in celebration.

Maya Nahual: Kej

Kej represents the four pillars of the sky and the earth. It may sustain community living and strenghten the mind. The deer brings grace and abundance.

WOLF

Freedom

Sharp Intelligence

Expressions of Instincts

Chaos and Fierceness

"A fight is going on inside me," he said to the boy.

"It is a terrible fight and it is between two wolves. One is evil - he is anger, envy, sorrow, regret, greed, arrogance, self-pity, guilt, resentment, inferiority, lies, false pride, superiority, and ego." He continued, "The other is good - he is joy, peace, love, hope, serenity, humility, kindness, benevolence, empathy, generosity, truth, compassion, and faith. The same fight is going on inside you - and inside every other person, too."

The grandson thought about it for a minute and then asked his grandfather,

"Which wolf will win?"

The old Cherokee simply replied, "The one you feed."□

Cherokee Saying

Few animals on Earth evoke such strong emotions as the wolf, or have suffered so much as a result of misunderstanding. In spite of its fierce reputation, it is a shy, intelligent and elusive creature. Wolf folktales abound, shrouded in mists of fear, admiration, awe and loathing. In hunter-gatherer societies, the wolf was often afforded respect for its incredible senses and hunting prowess; but with the rise of agriculture, and the threat to livestock that wolves often presented, conflicts with humans grew.

Its Gaelic names were Luh, Madadh Alluidh, and sometimes Mac Tire, meaning 'earth's son-. In Scotland, and indeed throughout Northern Europe and America, it was hunted ruthlessly, and eradicated from many areas. In Scotland, as early as the 2nd Century BC, King Dorvadilla decreed that anyone who killed a wolf would be rewarded with an ox, and in the 15th Century James the First of Scotland ordered the eradication of wolves in the kingdom. 'Last wolf' legends are found in many parts of Scotland, although the very last was allegedly killed in 1743, near the River Findhorn by a stalker named MacQueen. However, the historic accuracy of this story is dubious.

The images conveyed in wolf folktales vary: in many they are depicted as ruthless and fierce; in others they have an image of nobility and loyalty. In Norse Mythology, the Fenrir was a symbol of chaos who eventually swallows Odin whole. However, the wolf was also associated with warriors, and Odin had two wolves as loyal companions.

We are all familiar with tales such as Little Red Riding Hood and The Three Little Pigs. It is interesting that much European folklore portrays the wolf as a threat to humans. In contrast, there are a number of folktales with the theme of human children being raised by wolves. The Roman story of Romulus and Remus, and of course Mowgli in Kipling's The Jungle Book, are classic examples. Such stories reflect the strong maternal instinct attributed to wolves, and wolves generally had a positive image in Roman culture.

In Scottish folklore there are a number of tales of the Wolf and Fox. These tend to convey the Wolf as somewhat more gullible than the cunning Fox. In one tale Fox tricks Wolf out of a whole keg of butter, and in another Fox's trickery results in Wolf losing his tail.

Wolves were known to dig up dead human bodies and for this reason corpses were often buried on islands, such as Handa off the north-west coast of Scotland. The church often associated them with the devil, giving even stronger incentive for their eradication.

Werewolf legends were particularly prevalent in parts of Eastern Europe until very recently, Werewolf myths have been around perhaps even longer than those associated with vampires and other creatures. For example, Ancient Greek mythology tells of Lycaon, a man transformed into a wolf after eating human flesh. Furthermore, the word werewolf is thought to be derived from the Old English were, meaning "man." While the specific attributes of werewolves vary across different cultures, the beast itself is generally the same: a part-man, part-wolf creature of the night which preys on humans.

Wolves figure prominently in the mythology of nearly every Native American tribe. In most Native cultures, Wolf is considered a medicine being associated with courage, strength, loyalty, and success at hunting. Like bears, wolves are considered closely related to humans by many North American tribes, and the origin stories of some Northwest Coast tribes, such as the Quileute and the Kwakiutl, tell of their first ancestors being transformed from wolves into men. In Shoshone mythology, Wolf plays the role of the noble Creator god, while in Anishinabe mythology a wolf character is the brother and true best friend of the culture hero. Among the Pueblo tribes, wolves are considered one of the six directional guardians, associated with the east and the colour white. The Zunis carve stone wolf fetishes for protection, ascribing to them both healing and hunting powers.

Wolves are also one of the most common clan animals in Native American cultures. Tribes with Wolf Clans include the Creek, the Cherokee, the Chippewa, Lenape, Shawnee and Menominee, the Huron and Iroquois tribes, the Pueblo tribes of New Mexico, and Northwest Coast tribes like the Tlingit, Tsimshian, and Kwakiutl. Wolf was an important clan crest on the Northwest Coast and can often be found carved on totem poles. The wolf is also the special tribal symbol of several tribes and bands, such as the Munsee Delaware, the Mohegans, and the Skidi Pawnee. Some eastern tribes, like the Lenape and Shawnee, have a wolf dance among their tribal dance traditions.

The Legend of the Tlatoani Mocuitlachnehnequi is one of the oldest in the Aztec lore. It tells about a mysterious man known only as Cuetlachtli, which is translated among the people into "Wolf". Cuetlachtli appeared one day in the northeast city of El Tajín. He stood in the city centre and declared himself the new king, and that any and all who opposed him may step forward and challenge him for the right to lead the people. El Tajín's own King Milintica, the third son of Mixcoatl and leader of the cult of Quetzalcoatl, came forth. King Milintica called upon the "feathered serpent" to smite the stranger, but Cuetlachtli transformed into a wolf and man, killing King Milinitca and claiming the throne. So began the rule of Cuetlachtli, the Tlatoani Mocuitlachnehnequi. He was said to have come from the north, from Aztlán, the ancestral home of the Nahua. He was many centuries old, said to have been born atop a great mound. His ancestors were hunters, walking as man, becoming wolves as the sun set. The powers he possessed were unlike all seen before. No sorcerer, his equal and no warrior his superior. His followers were given his blood to make them walking wolves. It was an honour bestowed on those who could prove their worth. The reign of Tlatoani Mocuitlachnehnequi lasted many years.

In Mesoamerican lore, wolves are rarely represented and for Mayans wolves and dogs can evoke similar feelings. Totem wolf symbols recall deep faith, passion and profound understanding.

SCORPION

Death and Revenge
Fire and Transformation
Psyche
Preparedness
Dream Realm

"Artemis made Orion her companion; he guarded the goddess and he served her. Imprudent words incite the anger of gods: 'There is no beast,' he said, 'I cannot beat.' Gaia the Earth, unleashed a scorpion. Its urge was to stab the goddess of twins with its hooked stingers. Orion blocked it. Leto joined him to the bright stars, and said, 'Receive your reward for service."

Ovid

According to Ancient Greek mythology Zeus' son, Orion the Hunter, was killed by a scorpion produced by the Goddess Artemis after he had raped her. The basis of much of this attention to scorpions was fear, scorpions caused death with seemingly little effort.

In Syria, where the province of Commagene had the scorpion on one of its coins about 100 AD, it was so feared that in some places it was allowable to kill scorpions even on the sabbath, and even if they had not initiated an attack.

Scorpions also feature in ancient Chinese writings where they are linked with the toad, the centipede, the snake and the spider to form the Wu Tu or 5 poisonous animals. Much later the great Chinese encyclopaedia of 10 000 volumes produced in Peking in 1726 devoted 14 pages to scorpions.

All the ancient Greek and Roman scholars such as Aristotle and Pliny wrote of scorpions with varying degrees of accuracy.

114

For a period of about 300 hundred years from the early 1300s to late 1500s Christians often used the scorpion as an emblem for the Jewish people to symbolize perfidy.

Pliny believed in a number of cures for the effects of the scorpion sting including Aconite and Basil. This was still being reported in the 17th century. In the 16th century John Lyly writes that "By Basil the Scorpion is engendered; and by means of the same herb destroyed"

Many ancient myths about scorpions were still being retold until relatively modern times, among these was the belief that a scorpion surrounded by a ring of fire would sting itself to death, as scorpions are immune to their own stings this is highly unlikely.

The Chaldeans (Babylonia) grouped the major stars in the night sky into 12 constellations, one of these was Scorpio containing the bright red star Anteres, this is an indication of how potent a force the scorpion had become in people's minds 4 000 years ago. The 12 houses of the Zodiac in Astrology are derived from these star configurations and Scorpio is still among them. No insect has aspired to this claim though another arthropod has i.e. Cancer the Crab. Scorpions have played an important role in the mythology of people who live with them since the earliest times.

The warrior-god Sadrafa is depicted on a stelae from a temple of Bel, Palmyra dated to AD 55 with his attributes the scorpion and the serpent. He is however a much older mythological figure than this, being a forerunner of the Iranian Mithras by which time however he had lost his association with scorpions. In an ancient Persian legend Mithras the Persian god of light sacrificed the sacred bull in order that his blood might fertilize the universe thus creating life. However the evil Ahriman in order to destroy this life sent a scorpion to sting the bull on the testicles. Mithras remained a popular god throughout the Mediterranean area, particularly with Roman soldiers and was actively worshipped until about 500 AD. The scorpion is frequently seen as the agent of the devil.

In ancient Egypt representations of scorpions are frequently found on tombs and monuments. There is a section in the 'Ebers papyrus' entitled "How to Rid the House of Scorpions" and scorpions are mentioned in several passages in the 'Book of the Dead' as well as in the Talmud and the

Bible Old Testament. In Hebrew ancient history the scorpion was the emblem of the tribe of Dan. There is also a character 'Scorpion Man' guardian of Mount Mashu the place of sunrise and sunset in the Gilgamesh epic. This character later plays a role in the Babylonian Creation Tablets (650 BC) when he is one of the 11 mighty helpers that assisted Tiamat the mother of creation in overcoming her loathsome offspring. Images of the Scorpion-man were used in artistry and a fine extant example is a harp found in the Royal Necropolis of Ur from around 2 600 BC. The Egyptians also had a scorpion-goddess called Selkit or Serqet who was 'friend of the dead' and whose image often adorned artifacts relating to the mummification of the dead. She is sometimes depicted with a stylised scorpion on her head. More commonly people in Egypt believed until relatively recent times that scorpions originated from the bodies of dead crocodiles. While in Europe they believed that dead crabs turned into scorpions.

A scorpion wheel charm is associated with a (Tibetan Buddhist) Nyingma Yamantaka practice.

In Tibet in the fire puja of Vajradaka who is a fierce and wrathful deity invoked to purify negative actions, black sesame seeds are used to represent problems and regrets. They are arranged into the shape of a scorpion which is then consumed by fire as practitioners visualize all physical, psychological, emotional hindrances being annihilated compassionately by the deity who joyously devours them for us.

The fascination or threatening gesture (Skt. tarjini mudra) consists of a fist with forefinger and little finger extended; it is called the "forefinger-scorpion gesture". Legend says that when the apostate king Langdarma was attempting to suppress Buddhism in Tibet, mahasiddha Nubchen Sangyé Yeshé terrified him by using the gesture to create a scorpion apparition "as big as nine yaks" that appeared above the king.

Begtse is a Mongol war god that legend says, converted to Buddhism in the 16th-century at the sight of the Dalai Lama's transformation into Chenrezi, the Bodhisattva of Compassion. As a consequence, he became a symbol of pacification.

"He is represented with all the ornaments of the Dharmapala, brandishing a sword in his right hand, the handle of which is in the shape of a scorpion. His left hand holds the orange heart of an enemy near his mouth, clutching at the same time a bow and an arrow. He tramples upon the corpse of a man with his left foot and the carcass of a horse with his right foot. His three eyes are full of fury directed at the enemies of the dharma."

In the Americas generally the scorpion evokes the magical power of self-defence and the ability to perceive the threats.

Scorpions are found in 3-dimensional effigies in obsidian of Maya artifacts. On a few vases scorpions are incised or painted. Scorpions are part of Mayan cosmology since Maya astronomers recognized the scorpion constellation.

MONKEY

Cleverness
Playfulness and Joy
Greed
Childbirth
Responsability

Monkeys are common characters in the folklore of Mexican, Central American, and South American Indian tribes. Most often monkeys appear as trickster characters, using their cleverness to outwit other animals, humans, or even monsters. In the mythology of some South American tribes, monkey is a more serious figure whose curiosity or misbehaviour brings woe to humanity.

Monkey lore in India dates from before 500 BC. One of the most popular Hindu gods is Hanuman the Monkey, in some tales said to be an incarnation of Shiva. He is revered for his bravery, strength, loyalty, devotion, and dedication to justice. His tale and heroic exploits are told in both the Ramayana and the Mahabharata. It is common to chant the name of Hanuman when one needs heavenly intervention. Every year, his birthday is celebrated "on the full-moon day of Chaitra (April) at sunrise."

Monkeys in general are revered in several parts of India, for bearing the likeness of Hanuman. He is connected to the sun, the wind, and thunder.

Monkey lore in China predates Buddhism, for the Monkey appears in the Chinese Zodiacal beliefs, believed by scholars to date to around 1100BC. In some parts of China, the Monkey is worshipped as the "Great Sage Equal to Heaven."

In Chinese mythology, the monkey god was Sun-Wukong, the Monkey King, a trickster god. He is the hero of the 16th-century Chinese book

"Journey to the West".

Monkey lore in Japan took hold after the arrival of Buddhism (mid-6th century AD) and is tied to Japanese Shinto-Buddhism. The monkey was alternately a messenger to the gods or a physical manifestation of a god. In folklore and geomancy beliefs, the Monkey was thought to protect against demons as well as disease and is a patron of fertility, safe childbirth, and harmonious marriages.

For Native Americans monkeys are often related to natural disasters, particularly floods, sometimes are said to incarnate nightmares and fears. According to the legend of the Tcetin, or Monkey People. Monkeys are legendary humanoid creatures with tails. They lived in trees and caves. They were said to be enemies of humans. Their English name is a bit of a misnomer "Cet'aeni" and "Tcetin" are Athabaskan words for monkeys, but only in the modern era (no monkeys have ever lived in Alaska.) The names literally translate simply as "Tailed Ones."

Iwarrika is a mythological monkey from the Akawaio and other Caribbean tribes of South America. He is a trickster figure noted for his intelligence but also his laziness, disobedience, greed, and insatiable curiosity. Iwarrika is blamed for accidentally flooding the earth by disturbing a dam built by the benevolent demigod Sigu, either because of the monkey's inherent curiosity or because he was trying to steal food from Sigu. The name "Iwarrika" literally means "Monkey" in the Akawaio language (in particular it refers to the weeping capuchin).

The Mayans of Guatemala and Mexico worshiped a howler monkey god (sometimes depicted as twin-gods), who was the patron of the arts; music, scribes and sculptors. In the Mayan Calendar, the Howler Monkey corresponds to knowledge of history and rituals, as well as prophecy. There is a fabled "Ciudad Blanca" in Honduras, dedicated to the Monkey God, but so far its location is unknown—it is mentioned in pre-Columbian Toltec and Maya texts as "The ancient place where the aurora originates."

In Aztec mythology of Mexico, the monkey was connected to the sun, and was guarded by Xochipilli, the god of flower, fun, and fertility.

Maya Nahual: B'atz'

Dreaming about monkeys for Mayans is a call for creativity and regeneration. B'atz' will support the process of knowledge and innovation with an inquisitive mind.

LIZARD

Fortune

Resurrection

Collective Unconscious

Masculine Force

Survival

Control in Dreams

"In the parched path I have seen the good lizard

(one drop of crocodile) meditating.

With his green frock-coat of an abbot of the devil,

his correct bearing and his stiff collar,

he has the sad air of an old professor.

Those faded eyes of a broken artist,

how they watch the afternoon in dismay!"

Federico Garcia Lorca, The Old Lizard

The various myths reveal the association of certain sacred reptiles with the supernatural and with so-called magical powers. These themes are encountered among civilizations millennia in the past to our own present culture.

The behavioural pattern of the lizard has inspired various beliefs, myths and legends associated with the Sun. In Egypt, it is said that in spring the lizards will climb an eastward facing wall and look to the east. When the Sun rises, the lizard's sight and the sight of some blinded person, will is returned.

Lizards have been associated with extreme heat in the Near East and Australia, the aboriginal believed that the sky would fall if you killed one.

In ancient Egypt and Greek symbolism the lizard represented divine wisdom and good fortune. This was especially true of the reverence for Serapes and Hermes.

In Roman mythology, lizards supposedly sleep through the winter and so symbolize both death and resurrection. Early Christianity associated the lizard with the devil and with evil. While on the Pacific islands of Polynesia and Maoris lizards are revered as a "heaven god."

The Maori of New Zealand are well to the front as upholders of these singular beliefs. Generally speaking lizards were dreaded by all Polynesians, and the Maori carried this feeling to the extent of attributing misfortune, calamities, death, to lizards. One explanation of this belief is that the lizard represents Whiro, and Whiro personifies darkness and death; a Maori belief was that evil spirits in lizard form entered bodies of men and consumed their vitals, so causing death. When an expert was called in to treat the case he would pose as an exorcist and expel the malignant spirit from the body of the sufferer. Curiously enough the Maori dread of lizards did not always extend to the tuatara, the largest species thereof, for it was an article of food in pre-European times; this custom may not have been universal but it was certainly widespread.

Some wise men have told us that the common green lizard, the moko kakariki (Naultinus elegans) did not originate on earth, it just appeared from space. This looks like an offshoot of the myth concerning flying lizards. The Tuhoe folk said that the tree lizard develops from a kind of iro (maggot or worm) that is found in the nest of the tihe bird (Pogonornis cincta), while the iro from which the koeau species of lizard is developed is found in the nests of the kaka (Nestor meridionalis), and this iro is light-coloured.

Another reference to a flying lizard is in the following remark of a Takitimu native—"This lizard, the moko kakariki, is a supernatural creature. Tamaiwaho reared it when he and Tane went to Tiritiri-o-matangi, he brought it with him as a pet. When he reached Papa [the earth] then Peketua cherished it, and he deferred to it as a supernatural being or demon. So it was that this lizard attained the power of flying through space."

Lizards play positive roles in the folklore of many Native American tribes. In Plains Indian tribes, lizards are associated with healing and survival, and also with masculinity. In some Plains tribes, a newborn boy's umbilical cord was sewn into an amulet in the shape of a lizard to ensure his health and strength. Today, many Cheyenne people still consider it bad luck to kill a lizard. In the mythology of some California Indian tribes, such as the Pomo, Lizard was one of the major figures of creation, who made humans partially in his image.

In South Western tribes, horned lizards (sometimes called "horny-toads" in English) are considered sacred medicine animals; Gila monster (a type of large poisonous desert lizard) features as a powerful hero in Navajo and other legends. In other tribes, lizards are associated with protection (especially of children), prosperity, renewal, and good luck.

Some Mexican myths tells how the basilisk, a type of lizard, acquired the crest on its head. The Lord of the Woods announced that he would give a special hat to the animal that won a race. Most of the animals refused to compete, protesting that Big Deer was bound to win. However, to the amusement of all, the little basilisk said that it would race on one condition: all the animals had to close their eyes at the start of the race. The Lord of the Woods agreed, and Big Deer and the basilisk took off toward the stone that was their goal. When Big Deer arrived, he slowed down, thinking that he must have passed the basilisk long before. But to his surprise, as he prepared to sit on the stone, he found the basilisk there before him. The Lord of the Woods awarded the hat to the basilisk because he knew that the little creature had cleverly grabbed Big Deer's tail at the starting point and ridden it to the stone.

Maya Nahual: Imox

The psychic characteristics inherent in the lizard teach those with this medicine how to awaken their own abilities by making choices that honour every part of one's life. When lizard appears it signifies a need to go within and analyse your present reality and once done, move with confidence and conviction out into the world of new beginnings.

DOLPHIN

Sacrifice
Honour
Bonding
Fraternity

"The ecstatic waters laugh because
Their cries are sweet and strange,
Through their ancestral patterns dance,
And the brute dolphins plunge
Until, in some cliff-sheltered bay
Where wades the choir of love
Proffering its sacred laurel crowns,
They pitch their burdens off."
W.B. Yeats

Dolphins have been viewed as somehow magical for millennia by humans. They're one of the only animals that appear to play, leaping out of the water and doing tricks, and the bottlenose dolphin even seems to grin widely at everything. It was inevitable that such a remarkable animal also collected a remarkable mythology that extends through today.

The first culture that seems to have mythology associated with the dolphin was the Minoan, a seafaring people in the Mediterranean. They left few written records, but they did leave beautiful murals on the walls of their palaces, murals that show the importance of dolphins in their mythology.

Because they were strongly associated with Poseidon by the later Greeks, this probably explains why the sea god was so often surrounded by dolphins. In one myth about Poseidon, dolphin messengers were sent to bring him a nymph he loved, who he later married. As a reward, he set the dolphin in the sky as a constellation. And he was constantly accompanied by dolphins among other sea creatures.

This wasn't the last time the Greeks associated dolphins with romance. Aphrodite is often depicted with dolphins, riding them or being accompanied by them. Later, the god Dionysus transformed the way dolphins were perceived in Greek literature. He was set upon while at sea by a band of pirates. Instead of simply destroying the sea raiders, he transformed them into a pod of dolphins, charging them to rescue any distressed sailors in the ocean. Dolphins, in Greek culture, were often rescuers of humans, probably because they like to bring things to the surface and, well, because there's some really good evidence that they do indeed purposely rescue people in danger.

Byzantine sailors, Arab sailors, Chinese and European explorers, all had tales of dolphins rescuing sailors or ships in trouble. Dolphins could predict calm seas. And a ship accompanied by dolphins was sure to find safe harbour, fair weather, and following seas. Just as with an albatross, it was terrible luck to harm a dolphin.

Porpoises and dolphins are often confused with each other in English translations of Native American mythology. The "dolphin clan" and "dolphin totem" of the Tlingit and other coastal Alaskan tribes are actually Dall's porpoises, for example. (Some true dolphins, like the striped dolphin, do live as far north as Alaska, but the Tlingit have a different name for them.) Dolphins and porpoises are closely related to each other, and in some tribes (particularly tribes of the California coast) the same word is used to refer to both kinds of animals.

In any case, Native American tribes living near the oceans, like coastal cultures all over the world, have many stories about dolphins and porpoises helping people by carrying them to shore in rough waters or driving away menacing sharks. In some California Indian legends, dolphins are said to have been transformed from humans, and serve as special protectors of the tribe. (Some tribes forbid the eating of dolphin meat for this reason; others, like the Chumash, believe that dolphins intentionally sacrifice themselves to hunters in order to feed the people, and hold special Dolphin Dances in their honour.) And in South America, Amazon River dolphins (also known as "pink dolphins" or "boto dolphins") are regarded with fear and awe by some indigenous tribes, who believe the dolphins to be powerful shapeshifting sorcerers that may seduce women or drive men insane.

A legend from Chumash people of Limuw Island explains that Hutash (Mother Earth) told the people to go across the rainbow bridge and to fill the whole world with people. So the Chumash people started to go across the bridge. Some of them got across safely, but some people made the mistake of looking down. It was a long way down to the water, and the fog was swirling around. They became so dizzy that some of them fell off the rainbow bridge, down through the fog, into the ocean. Hutash felt very badly about this because she told them to cross the bridge. She did not want them to drown. To save them, she turned them into dolphins. Now the Chumash call the dolphins their brothers and sisters.

ABOUT THE AUTHOR

An Italian molecular biologist and a visionary alchemist, studying medicinal plants and entheogens, and working for many years in international co-operation projects throughout Asia, Africa and Latin America.
During her experience with indigenous people living in an immaculate rainforest in Panamá, she started an ongoing research on states of consciousness, ethnobotany and human brain evolution, specifically focused on plants and shamanism as a natural ring connection.

The urge of a shared, worldwide accessible knowledge gave spiritual insight to her journey and brought her to create *Alquimia*, an unconventional centre based on entheogenic education where pure concepts of sustainability, reconnection to nature and scientific noesis are oneness. She currently lives in Guatemala.

From the same author: 'The Hidden Maya Forest - Sacred and Medicinal Plants and Rituals of Guatemala".

Made in the USA
Middletown, DE
20 October 2020